Athena Critical Guides: Beloved

A Level Study Guide

	Page
General Introduction	**3**
Part One: Contexts of Production	**6**
1.1 Introducing Contexts: Toni Morrison	7
1.2 Historical Contexts: The Modern Medea	14
1.3 Social Contexts: *'Sixty Million and More...'*	21
1.4 Literary Contexts: Slave narratives and the supernatural	29
Part Two: Introducing Critical Approaches	**39**
2.1 Narrative, Structure and Style	40
2.2 Characterisation	45
2.3 Themes and Symbolism	53
2.4 Settings - Crossing Boundaries	66
2.5 The 'Other'	70
Part Three: Textual Commentary and Analysis	**72**
3.1 Part I: Chapters 1-8	73
3.2 Part I: Chapters 9-18	83
3.3 Part II: Chapters 19-25	92
3.4 Part III: Chapters 26-28	102
Part Four: Contexts of Reception	**108**
4.1 Critical Reception: Contemporary Reviews	109
4.2 Genre-Based and Structuralist Approaches	118
4.3 Psychoanalytical and Gendered Readings	134
4.4 Postmodern and Post-Colonial Readings	138
Appendices	**145**
Examples of Examination Tasks	146
References for Wider Reading	147

General Introduction

Advanced Level Study Guide: Toni Morrison's *Beloved*

This Study Guide has been written to assist the learner in understanding Toni Morrison's text *Beloved* in conjunction with relevant literary and critical contexts.

This Study Guide will support critical reflection and careful examination of Toni Morrison's *Beloved*, while fostering appreciation for the contexts in which it was produced and received, along with the historical events which inspired the narrative.

Considered by many to be Morrison's masterpiece, *Beloved* remains a popular text for students of Advanced Literature. The novel is also of interest as a text for learners undertaking independent extended projects and non-examined assessments.

This Study Guide is also suitable for those with a general interest in Morrison's work.

Aims and objectives of Advanced Level GCE English Literature

When engaging with literary texts in Advanced Level study, you will be required to show knowledge and understanding of:

- how writers use language, form and structure to shape meanings and evoke responses in the reader

- how to make connections and explore relationships between a range of literary texts

- the contexts in which texts have been produced and received, and how these contexts influence meaning

- ways of reading and experiencing texts critically and creatively

- how attitudes and values are expressed in texts

- how to communicate fluently, accurately and effectively

- use critical concepts and terminology with discrimination.

Who is this study guide for?

This Study Guide is intended to offer support for those learners who undertake an AS or A level qualification in English Literature or English Language and Literature. These qualification pathways are offered by most examination boards, and this resource is primarily designed to assist those who are studying this topic for the GCE qualification, but it may also provide support for those embarking on undergraduate study of *Beloved*.

This study guide will help to lay a sound foundation for those who go on to study English Literature and American prose at a higher (degree) level, as well as appeal to those who are interested in learning more about the work of Toni Morrison and, in particular, *Beloved*.

About Athena Online Education

Athena Online Education comprises of a specialist team of professional course writers based in the UK, Greece and Spain. All course writers are highly-qualified subject specialists and are experienced teachers, lecturers and course writers, as well as being experienced and current examination assessors for the main examination boards, including CIE, AQA, OCR and Edexcel.

Editions of the Text

A-level examination boards do not currently recommend a set edition of Toni Morrison's *Beloved*. Any edition is valid and may be used by a learner.

The following edition is commonly available and is the version cited in this guide;

Morrison, Toni   *Beloved*. Vintage Classics; London, 2007.

A note on character names

Some names and references in the novel do not use capital letters or standard punctuation. This is most notable in descriptions and recounts of events involving 'schoolteacher' and the 'crawling? already' baby. This has been a deliberate choice by Morrison and should be observed when writing about these characters.

Examination Boards

This product is designed to be used as a study aid to support learners in their preparation for the following examination units;

EDEXCEL Literature 8ET02 Prose
EDEXCEL Literature 9ET02 Prose

It can also provide useful support for non-examined assessment units, including:

AQA A 7712 Literature Independent Critical Study: Texts Across Time
AQA B 7717 Theory and Independence
CCEA Unit A2 3: Internal Assessment
EDUQAS Literature Component 4 Prose Study
OCR Component 3: Post-1900 Literature
WJEC Literature Component 5 Prose Study
WJEC Language and Literature Component 5 Genre Study

Using this guide

This guide aims to support the reader in extended study of the novel *Beloved*. The text is considered in the wider contexts in which it was written and has been received. The guide is presented in four parts:

Part One, Contexts of Production, considers the writer's life and times, with a focus on significant historical, social and literary contexts.

Part Two introduces some critical approaches, including exploration of; narrative, characterisation, structure, key themes and relevant critical ideas.

Part Three provides detailed commentary and analysis of each chapter, with relevant background information and reading tasks to enhance understanding.

Part Four, Contexts of Reception, examines how the text was initially received, as well as providing a critical overview of a range of interpretations and approaches.

Direct quotations from the novel appear in *italics.*

Part One:
Introducing Critical Approaches

1.1 Introducing Contexts: Toni Morrison

1.2 Historical Contexts: The Modern Medea

1.3 Social Contexts: 'Sixty Million and More...'

1.4 Literary Contexts: Slave narratives and the supernatural

1.1 Introducing Contexts: Toni Morrison

In this section we will;

- *Demonstrate understanding of the significance and influence of the contexts in which Beloved was written and received*
- *Explore the life and literary career of Toni Morrison*
- *Explore connections across literary texts and contexts*
- *To consider wider social and historical contexts*

Introducing Contexts

When approaching a text at A level, students should consider the contexts of reception and production, and how these may affect the way texts are interpreted. Some of the contexts which may prove relevant to the study of the novel are outlined below. These include:

- *contexts of writing*
- *contexts of reading*
- *contexts of time and place*
- *social and cultural contexts*

Social and cultural contexts and contexts of time and place will be discussed throughout the detailed commentary and analysis sections.

As part of your A Level study you are required to consider the wider social, historical and literary contexts of a text, that is, the world in which it is produced and received.

Contexts of Writing: Biographical Contexts

We can begin with a biographical outline of key dates in a writer's life. Facts such as the dates of publication of particular works can provide some sense of the writer's literary development or changing concerns.

Toni Morrison

Morrison sought to face the issues of race and heritage through genuine human relationships. Born Chloe Wofford, she herself came from Ohio, where *Beloved* is set. Her own grandfather moved from the poverty and ingrained racism of Kentucky to farm, and work as a tradesman. Her father George Wofford was a sharecropper in Georgia before moving to weld in northern ship yards. Wofford's experiences left him bitter and racist, failing to trust any word or gesture of a white man. Morrison's mother Ranah Wills Wofford had a gentler view and encouraged questioning of inequalities.

Morrison was close to the older generations of women in her family. They both influenced and inspired. Religion was an important foundation to life, alongside oral storytelling. Morrison's family taught her about the Underground Railroad and other stories of the South after Reconstruction, mainly passed down from her maternal grandparents John Solomon and Ardelia Willis, who emigrated from Alabama in 1912. The women in Morrison's life inspired the strong characters in many of her novels.

Education and Career

Morrison wrote stories and poetry from a young age. She undertook study of Latin at her high school and wished to go forward to obtain a college degree. It was at Harvard University in Washington DC that Morrison changed her name from Chloe to Toni, an abbreviation of her Catholic confirmation name Antony. She gained her BA in 1953 gaining a Masters in English at Cornell in 1955.

As well as producing fiction, Morrison has published a wide range of critical writing. She held various positions as Lecturer and Professor of Literature in leading American universities. Morrison taught in Texas Southern and Howard universities in the later 1950s. Morrison left education to write in 1962. In 1965 she returned to Lorain, Ohio after the end of her marriage. Here she began to write fiction.

From 1965-1983 Morrison worked as a textbook editor in New York. She used writing as a way of addressing isolation. In 1968 she published *The Bluest Eye*. By 1968 Morrison had become a Senior Editor and was seeing her own work published.

In 1969 she returned to working as a professor in New York State. 1973 saw the publication of *Sula*. The novel contrasted the experiences of two women and their relationships with the wider community. The exploration of rebellion and conformity would become a theme in later works.

Morrison worked to edit *The Black Book* in 1974. This was an important collection of texts and documents charting black culture and experience in America. Morrison felt this provided her with an education and some of the artefacts fed into her writing.

The Black Book (1974)

Morrison edited the historical anthology *The Black Book* (1974). It was published at a point when the Black Power movement of the 1960s and 1970s was in danger of being constrained to rhetoric and suggesting historical erasure and denial of the past. In celebrating a few great men, Black Power narratives were possibly overlooking the ordinary heroics of normal people who survived slavery.

Morrison 'answers back' with *Beloved* and in doing so questions the romanticism of African and American past.

Morrison completed and published *Song of Solomon* in 1977. The novel has a male protagonist and made use of magic realism with characters escaping through flight. Milkman Dead explores his roots and African American tradition.

She continued to combine writing with visiting lecturer posts in Yale and Bard. Tar Baby was published in 1981. Morrison produced a commissioned drama inspired by the race murder of 14-year-old Emmett Tell, *'Dreaming Emmett'* in 1986, with *Beloved* published the following year in 1987.

Toni Morrison, taken at *Westpoint Academy Lecture 2013*

For many, *Beloved* (1987) is Morrison's masterpiece. It is the first novel in a trilogy chronicling the impact of traumatic events on African American communities over the past 150 years. It is based on the story of Margaret Garner, a mother who murdered her child rather than have her taken back into slavery, which Morrison encountered when compiling *The Black Book* (1974). In the novel, the mother and her remaining daughter are haunted by the memory of the dead child, and the novel also presents the ways in which the horrors of slavery haunt African Americans, even when freedom has apparently been achieved.

Other notable and successful novels include *Jazz* (1992) and *Paradise* (1998), which form the second and third part of the trilogy. Morrison won the Nobel Prize for Literature following the publication of *Jazz* (1992), the story of a murder and betrayal drawing on jazz motifs in its free-flowing structure. *Paradise* returned to Ohio to focus on an act of violence and its effect on a group of women.

Morrison published *Love* in 2003. She presented another historical narrative in *A Mercy* (2008). The story is set in colonial Virginia in 1682 and looks at how various groups and communities sought to survive and hold power. *Home* (2012) has a male protagonist who is a Korean living in America seeking to rescue his sister from medical experimentation. *God Help the Child* (2015) reprised the themes of *The Bluest Eye* (1968), this time exploring the thoughts of a woman working in fashion who is constrained by memories of her mother's aversion to her dark skin.

Morrison continued to produce fiction and non-fiction alongside her teaching posts until her death in August 2019.

Awards

Morrison has won a number of literary awards, including the Pulitzer Prize in 1988 and the Nobel Prize in 1993. Her work is celebrated for its formal complexity while questioning wider issues relating to slavery, race, gender and historical memory. Morrison's work raises debates about the possibility of creating literature 'that is both aesthetically beautiful and politically engaged' (Peterson from *Introduction: Canonizing Toni Morrison,* Modern Fiction Studies, 39 (1993), p.465).

Morrison helped edit *The Black Book* in 1974. This collection of documents and photographs was published at a point when the Black Power movement which emerged in the 1960s was in danger of being constrained by rhetoric and was suggesting historical erasure or denial of the past. In celebrating a few great men, Black Power movements were perhaps overlooking the ordinary heroics of those who survived slavery. *The Black Book* was designed to pay tribute to those experiences.

Morrison has won numerous academic and literary awards, and became the first black woman to be awarded the Nobel Prize for Literature in 1993.

Some key critical awards and appointments include:

1975   National Book Award.

1980   Appointment on National Council on the Arts. A range of other literary prizes including Book of the Month Club and the Wolf Book Award.

1981   Invited to American Writers' Congress

1988   *Beloved* gained nominations for Ritz-Hemingway, National Book Award and National Book Critics Circle. A high-profile campaign argued that Morrison had not won due to marginalisation of African-American literature.

1988   Pulitzer Prize for *Beloved*.

1993   Nobel Prize for Literature. Morrison was the only African American writer and one of the few women to have received the Nobel prize for literature. The announcement of her 1993 award cited her as a writer *'who, in novels characterised by visionary force and poetic import, gives life to an essential aspect of American reality'*.

> *'We die...That may be the meaning of life.*
>
> *But we do language. That may be the measure of our lives.'*
>
> Toni Morrison, **Nobel Acceptance Speech**

Morrison on writing

In her Nobel acceptance speech and other critical essays, Morrison emphasised the central importance of language *'partly as a system, partly as a living thing over which one has control, but mostly as an agency – as an act with consequences'*.

Morrison questioned the romanticism of the American and African past. She sought to challenge traditional stereotypes and to address the absence or marginalisation of African-American communities in traditional American literature. She saw fiction as a force for social change;

'Narrative is radical, creating us at the very moment it is being created ...'

As an educator and critical essay writer herself, Morrison also took part in numerous interviews during her career.

Paul Gilroy 'Living Memory: A Meeting with Toni Morrison'

Critical Reading: Paul Gilroy 'Living Memory: A Meeting with Toni Morrison' in *Small Acts: Thoughts on the Politics of Black Cultures* (1993)

Gilroy feels the novel has a focus on black women and motherhood. The narrative also served to explore 'the tension between the racial self and the racial community'. In *Beloved*, it is Sethe's sense of who she is as a mother which distances her from the community, who feel she is too proud. In his discussion with Toni Morrison she refutes the comparison between Margaret Garner and Medea, arguing Garner didn't kill her child 'because of some guy'. Women are the means and sources of production in the factory system of slavery, and Garner sought to remove her children from the system, particularly female children who will be seen as future producers.

Garner for Morrison is a 'classic example of a person determined to be responsible'. Margaret's actions show 'the indomitable power of slaves to assert their humanity in restricted circumstances'.

Gilroy thought *Beloved* 'aimed to place slavery back in the heart of Afro-America's political and literary culture'.

Beloved draws on the opposition of ideologies on history, property and kinship. Slaves for Morrison experienced the first truly modern difficulty in the middle of the nineteenth century, almost a century before the period deemed as modernist. Her central thesis is that modern life begins with slavery. Black women had difficulties we now deem as 'post-modern';

'Certain kinds of dissolution, the loss of and the need to reconstruct certain kinds of stability'.

Life as a slave meant losing any sense of self, as women lost their rights to be individuals, wives and mothers. In these situations, madness is required to avoid losing your mind. Slavery can be seen as a form of pathology rather than an ideology. Morrison feels slavery broke not just America but Europe. European slave traders 'had to dehumanise, not just the slaves but themselves'. Slavery made several wars possible, as the positioning of the opponent as 'other' is often driven by scientific racism.

Traditionally post modernism is explained as a reaction to the disintegration of twentieth century society after two world wars and the Holocaust. It is regarded as disillusionment with the 'grand narratives' of progress and enlightenment.

While the text is not wholly historical, it does address 'the recovery of historical memory'. Morrison notices that many post-modernists seem innocent. America is a country which erases its past or romanticizes it. African-American writers return to history because they feel responsibility.

Other interviews with Morrison

Toni Morrison notes that the richness of a text is the richness of interpretations brought by the reader. She gives the example of folk tales which can be 'passed on and somebody else can alter it later' (Darling, 1988).

There is a caution to remember with interviews and that is that authorial intention, while a clear indicator of what the writer is aiming to achieve, should still be treated as subjective rather than neutral fact.

Marsha Darling, 'In the Realm of Responsibility: Conversation with Toni Morrison', *Women's Review of Books*, March 1988.

Morrison identifies key areas of responsibility, namely the text as a response to history and the deaths occurring in relation to the Middle Passage, and the responsibility to produce a meaningful portrayal of an African-American mother's feelings towards their children in a time of slavery.

For Morrison, Beloved as a character functions on a number of levels. She can be seen as a spirit, literally the incarnation of the child returned from the dead. She could be a survivor from a ship. She could also be a victim of trauma, her language and preoccupations hinting at her troubled history. The references to 'over there' are vague enough to encompass the afterlife and a ship. Morrison insists 'both things are possible'. She hopes the reader may appreciate that 'the language of both experiences – death and the Middle Passages – is the same'.

The modern reader needs to take responsibility for those who have never had a history, those who did not survive. There is some criticism of freed slaves, who understandably in rushing away from slavery also rushed away from painful memories. Now, however, there needs to be recognition that in doing so they abandoned some of the responsibilities to the dead. However, it is not punishment or atonement that is called for. Memory must not be destructive – it must be possible to remember and to heal. Morrison terms this 'memory and re-memory'. In creating Sethe, Morrison is perhaps critiquing Margaret Garner's excess of maternal feeling. Slavery compelled her to extreme action as slavery denied motherhood, but there perhaps needs to be the persistent struggle to nurture without sacrificing self.

1.2 Historical Contexts: The 'Modern Medea'

In this section we will;

- *Demonstrate understanding of the significance and influence of the contexts in which Beloved was written and received*
- *Explore connections across literary texts and contexts*
- *To consider wider social and historical contexts*

Intertextuality: Margaret Garner, The 'Modern Medea'

Morrison took her inspiration for *Beloved* from a newspaper article detailing the tragic case of Margaret Garner, a runaway slave who took the extreme measure of killing one of her children rather than allow the family to be taken back into slavery.

'The Modern Medea – The Story of Margaret Garner' in *Harper's Weekly*

'A Visit to the Slave Mother Who Killed Her Child'

The following details are from the account given by Reverend P Bassett in the *American Baptist* on 12th February 1856, *'A Visit to the Slave Mother Who Killed Her Child'*.

As a Christian abolitionist, Bassett wrote trying to gain support and sympathy for the cause of 'that unfortunate woman'. He talked to Garner about her motivations and conveys 'that with regard to herself, she cared but little; but she was unwilling to have her children suffer as she had done'.

The reverend wonders if her act was a moment of madness. She explains to him that she viewed killing her children as a way of preventing future suffering. Rather than 'have them taken back to slavery, and be murdered by piece-meal'. Garner recalls her own experience of slavery as 'days of suffering…nights of unmitigated toil'.

The Reverend has a moral objection to slavery which is irresponsible in trying to wield power over other intelligent beings. While he sympathises with Garner's plight, he does find her assertion that her child is now far from trouble chilling and unsettling, yet recognises in her the 'passionate tenderness of a mother's love'.

Garner's mother-in-law was ambivalent regarding Margaret's extreme actions but tells the Reverend that 'under similar circumstances she would probably have done the same'.

Medea

A figure from Ancient Greek myth. Medea was a barbarian woman who was believed to be a sorceress. Jason brought her back to Greece as his wife where she was treated with suspicion as she was an outsider with dangerous powers.

When Jason cast her aside, she used sorcery to avenge herself. Euripides in his Greek tragedy 'Medea' tells how Medea sought revenge on Jason and murdered their children to assert power over him.

Differences from source material

Morrison cites Margaret Garner as a source but restricted her research to an 1856 article on the crime and how it was a direct result of the Fugitive Slave Law of 1850. While the abolitionists had presented the argument that Garner was a person rather than a piece of property, the Fugitive Act was upheld and she was remanded back into slavery. Morrison presents a version where Sethe has a degree of triumph over the law and is released.

Reconstruction Era Ohio was not the paradise it was assumed to be and Morrison can only present her narrative by 'imagining an alternative past'.

There are reasons for the changes Morrison made to Garner's story. The original records of the crime and trial made repeated reference to the paleness of the dead child, suggesting she was a product of rape. While still shocking, it would provide some rationale for the violence. Morrison seeks to complicate the reader's response as Sethe kills her child solely out of love.

Garner was tried for theft, with the child and adults treated as property. In *Beloved*, Sethe is released after a few months in prison, with her previous owners deciding she is too wild to take back. Morrison presents the killing as a result of Sethe's claim of motherhood and ownership. While clearly presenting the terrors of slavery, it is perhaps also a critique of a motherhood which seeks to claim another human. However, the reader is encouraged to sympathise with Sethe's pain and the reader accepts the notion of a mother trying to keep her children safe.

The critic Christopher Peterson feels the story is dominated by an idealized construction of maternal love. The community however see Sethe as a pariah, 'a sign of abjection and unintelligibility'. For them it does not look like love, more like pride and an unhealthy desire to have power.

The infanticide suggests proof of an animal nature to those who support racist ideologies, while the abolitionists see the deed as one of desperation and proof of slavery's evil. It can be argued that idealising the mother's act as pure love disavows the violence. Peterson finds that critical reception of the novel often fails to address 'the nexus of violence and kinship'.

While Margaret Garner herself was of mixed heritage, *Beloved* excludes any possibility of miscegenation in Sethe's family, although it is in evidence everywhere else in the text. Peterson wishes to examine this and notes;

'Like Beloved herself, miscegenation emerges as an absent presence that demands to be reckoned with'.

The earlier trauma of the nephews taking Sethe's milk is a sacrilege of her motherhood. Whiteness here contaminates and threatens her role as mother. There is a sense of mourning and otherness. Sethe 'disremembers', a form of 'dismembering'. She has been digested and later Beloved will digest her stories before being dismembered herself.

Sethe's family are the product of love and she tries to kill her children before the master can claim them. There is irony in her method providing a violent claim in itself, although Sethe proclaims it an act of pure love. The community cannot agree and even Paul D is stunned, reflecting that her love is 'too thick', an excessive and violent passion. This has echoes of the phrase 'blood is thicker than water' and there is a sense the town has perhaps been jealous that Sethe has managed to reunite with her children when they choose to turn away and not forewarn her of the approaching gang.

In the past Sethe has refused explanations which suggested she had an animal or violent reaction. She recalls an unconscious 'No!' and cannot explain her actions in rational terms. When she believes Beloved has returned to her in a living body, she is content, and decides that if her daughter is alive, she has never then had to give herself to the stonemason. Peterson counters that 'Sethe's body is always and irreducibly marked as a site of mourning'.

The community has a degree of belief in the Christian spirit world, yet Beloved is a demonic subversion of this as she is continually portrayed as an 'angry fleshy ghost'. Beloved is more than a daughter and a sister. She is a spirit who 'fails to contain the mourning she emblematizes'. The mourning without limits that she seeks to encourage links to the 'sixty million and more' souls unaccounted for and lost in the process of enslaving humans. Beloved frequently claims to be 'all' and 'more' than what others perceive her to be.

New Historicist critics would argue that history and the past is not unmediated. We always encounter it through texts; in this case a newspaper clipping inspired a novel. It is important to remember that while we encounter history through texts it is not the same as saying history is textual. It can be said that to take the historical position is to recognise history has competing representations and meanings. There is a realisation that as a modern novel *Beloved* cannot be 'authentic' but can explore the perspective of victims silenced in the past.

Introducing Critical Viewpoints: Adapted from Christopher Peterson (2008)
***Beloved*'s Claim**

The pivotal violence of Sethe's killing of her baby daughter highlights the opposition between the maternal claim and the slaveowner's claim of property. Murder returns Sethe's child to her. On her return, Beloved has her own claim on the living.

Kinship exists in opposition to slavery. Family ties are threatened and severed by arbitrary decisions made by slave owners. Peterson argues that both the parent and the slaveowner present claims that focus on the child as property. Children of slavery presented an intersection of property and kinship.

In later reparations slaves were able to claim compensation for property taken. It emerged that items were claimed as much as for the ways in which they linked to people they had loved as what the item was.

Tensions relating to property and kinship lend to violence erupting when 'the other...is reduced to the same'. Derrida considers the notion of kinship as the constant 'other' within self, while Levinas kinship is based on categorising by 'sameness'. Kinship has the possibility of violence. The real-life case of Margaret Garner was used to either support vile racist theory or to present her actions as divine mother love.

Homi Bhabha explains that Sethe 'regains through the presence of the child, the property of her own person. This knowledge comes as a kind of self-love that is also love of the other'.

Further Reading: '*Beloved's Claim*' Peterson, Christopher. *MFS Modern Fiction Studies*, Volume 52, Number 3, Autumn 2006, pp. 548-569

TASK: Introducing Critical Ideas

What do you understand Peterson means by 'the maternal claim'?

How is kinship or family threatened by slavery?

Looking back at the picture 'The Modern Medea' and Reverend Bassett's interview with Margaret Garner;

-in what ways can she be seen as 'other' or monstrous, and

-in what ways does she have sympathy as a mother?

Do you agree with Homi Bhabha that Sethe regains herself when Beloved returns?

Read the poem *The Slave Mother: A Tale of the Ohio* by Frances Ellen Watkins Harper, and answer the questions that follow:

I have but four, the treasures of my soul,
They lay like doves around my heart;
I tremble lest some cruel hand
Should tear my household wreaths apart.

My baby girl, with childish glance,
Looks curious in my anxious eye,
She little knows that for her sake
Deep shadows round my spirit lie.

My playful boys could I forget,
My home might seem a joyous spot,
But with their sunshine mirth I blend
The darkness of their future lot.

And thou my babe, my darling one,
My last, my loved, my precious child,
Oh! when I think upon thy doom
My heart grows faint and then throbs wild.

The Ohio's bridged and spanned with ice,
The northern star is shining bright,
I'll take the nestlings of my heart
And search for freedom by its light.

Winter and night were on the earth,
And feebly moaned the shivering trees,
A sigh of winter seemed to run
Through every murmur of the breeze.

She fled, and with her children all,
She reached the stream and crossed it o'er,
Bright visions of deliverance came
Like dreams of plenty to the poor.

Dreams! vain dreams, heroic mother,
Give all thy hopes and struggles o'er,
The pursuer is on thy track,
And the hunter at thy door.

Judea's refuge cities had power
To shelter, shield and save,
E'en Rome had altars, 'neath whose shade
Might crouch the wan and weary slave.

But Ohio had no sacred fane,
To human rights so consecrated,
Where thou may'st shield thy hapless ones
From their darkly gathering fate.

Then, said the mournful mother,
If Ohio cannot save,
I will do a deed for freedom,
Shalt find each child a grave.

I will save my precious children
From their darkly threatened doom,
I will hew their path to freedom
Through the portals of the tomb.

A moment in the sunlight,
She held a glimmering knife,
The next moment she had bathed it
In the crimson fount of life.

They snatched away the fatal knife,
Her boys shrieked wild with dread;
The baby girl was pale and cold,
They raised it up, the child was dead.

Sends this deed of fearful daring
Through my country's heart no thrill,
Do the icy hands of slavery
Every pure emotion chill?

Oh! if there is any honor,
Truth or justice in the land,
Will ye not, us men and Christians,
On the side of freedom stand?

Frances Ellen Watkins Harper (1825-1911) *'The Slave Mother (A Tale of Ohio)'*

Harper was an abolitionist and writer of novels, poems, and journalism. She was a free black woman and Temperance advocate. Her poem *'The Slave Mother'* is based on the case of Margaret Garner, and called others to join the crusade against the dishonour of slavery. The poem is presented in part as a dramatic monologue imagining Garner addressing her children. The verses from the perspective of the poet set the scene and later provide a moment of reflection on the difficulties Garner faced.

TASK: Exploring Harper's Poem *'The Slave Mother'*

How does Harper convey the mother's love for her children in the opening verses?

Why do you think the poet compares America to ancient Rome and Judea (a region now in modern Israel) in verse 9?

How does the mother hope to 'do a deed for freedom'? What does this tell us about Garner's experience of slavery?

In what way is the killing 'a deed of fearful daring'?

How does the poet want us to respond to Margaret Garner?

1.3 Social Contexts: *'Sixty Million and More...'* -The Legacy of Slavery

In this section we will;

- *Demonstrate understanding of the significance and influence of the contexts in which Beloved was written and received*
- *Explore connections across literary texts and contexts*
- *To consider wider social and historical contexts*

Representations of slavery

The 'Middle Passage':

This is the name given to the transatlantic route used by ships carrying captured Africans to enslavement on American plantations.

Some of Beloved's memories would seem to evoke the horror of these crossings.

Morrison presents a range of graphic and traumatic memories that indicate the horrors suffered by both males and females under a system of slavery. Where traditional slave narratives written in the nineteenth century referenced violence and violation in veiled allusions, Morrison's aim is to express the repressed stories, often in graphic detail.

Life as a slave on a plantation is explored directly through the memories and lived experiences of Sethe and Paul D, detailing both the relatively benign practices of Garner and the sadistic and horrifying debasement under the 'care' of schoolteacher. There are also stories presented from the perspectives of Baby Suggs, Stamp Paid and Ella which reveal the scale and range of mistreatment and abuse.

In *Beloved*, Morrison goes beyond creating empathy for the struggles and hardships of her female protagonist, to look at the legacy of slavery and the belief that the true victims of slavery number 'sixty million and more...'.

The epigraph at the start of the novel is taken from the Bible, Romans 9:25. This is a New Testament text with some echoes of the Old Testament. It perhaps suggests universal themes and problems when aiming to reclaim and repossess the past in the present. All should be remembered and 'be loved'.

The human cost of slavery

The 'sixty million and more' is a calculation of the human cost of slavery to those of African descent since the Colony of Virginia enslaved the first Africans to work in the plantations of the English colonies in August 1619. In the novel, Beloved's memories move back in time and present fragments of stories; of women being captured from their homes in Africa, of the horrendous and cramped conditions as slaves were transported on the slave ships of the 'Middle Passage' from West African nations to American plantations, of slaves being forced overboard to certain death at sea, of girls being held by officers or slave masters and being subjected to sexual abuse, and children being torn from their mothers. Once in America, the institution of slavery generated further victims, as women were used to breed more slaves and create future profit. Many of these victims have been lost and forgotten by history.

It is telling that in 2019, on the 400th anniversary of recorded enslavement of Africans, America and Britain are still facing challenges relating to the representation of slavery in history. There have been a number of public campaigns to remove or modify statues and plaques celebrating historical figures who gained significant wealth from the slave trade; there is also a need to represent the experiences of those who suffered enslavement. Museums documenting lynching and a living history plantation have been opened recently in Montgomery, Alabama and Whitney, Louisiana.

A free human

'cannot see things in the same light with the slave, because he does not and cannot look from the same point from which the slave does.'

Frederick Douglass (1855)

The Middle Passage

The Middle Passage was the second part of a triangular system of trade. Ships set out from European centres of wealth such as Britain, making their way to West African nations, where they then captured African men, women and children. It is calculated that 12.5 million people were taken on the transatlantic trade route to be forced into enslaved labour on American plantations. Around four million of these people did not survive, either dying of illness or drowning after being forced overboard

The goods produced on the plantations, such as sugar, wine, tobacco, coffee, tea, flour, grains, and timber, were sold back to consumers in American and Europe. Further money was made by exploiting agricultural technologies seen in West Africa, with additional finance generated by ship-building and the insurance and financing of trade expeditions. A number of families generated substantial wealth though links to the trade which spanned many generations. Simultaneously, generations of African and African-American communities were harmed by the institution of slavery.

Conditions on the slave ships of the 'Middle Passage'

By 1807 in England and 1808 in the United States it was unlawful to import slaves from Africa. Slaves could still be kept and new slaves could be bred in both countries. Navy patrols did stop suspected slave trading ships and returned human cargo to Africa. The following account was from Reverend Walsh, travelling with the navy patrol, who witnessed 517 slaves being returned from the *Feloz*, sadly not before 55 people had been thrown overboard by the slavers.

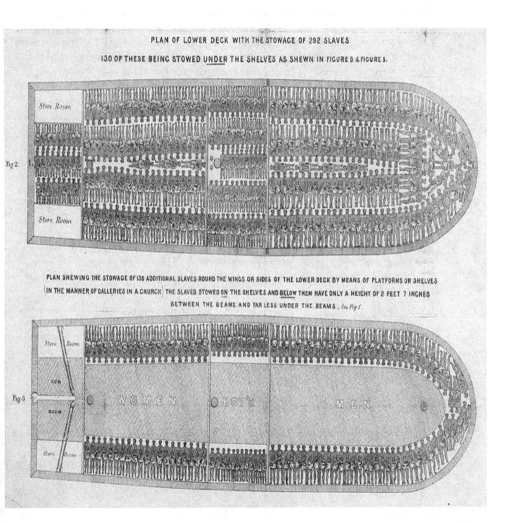

Diagram illustrating how slaves were transported

The following is from the eyewitness account of Reverend Walsh:

> *The slaves were all enclosed under grated hatchways between decks. The space was so low that they sat between each other's legs and [were] stowed so close together that there was no possibility of their lying down or at all changing their position by night or day. As they belonged to and were shipped on account of different individuals, they were all branded like sheep with the owner's marks of different forms. These were impressed under their breasts or on their arms, and, as the mate informed me with perfect indifference 'burnt with the red-hot iron.'*
>
> *Over the hatchway stood a ferocious-looking fellow with a scourge of many twisted thongs in his hand, who was the slave driver of the ship, and whenever he heard the slightest noise below, he shook it over them and seemed eager to exercise it. I was quite pleased to take this hateful badge out of his hand, and I have kept it ever since as a horrid memorial of reality, should I ever be disposed to forget the scene I witnessed.*
>
> *...Some, however, hung down their heads in apparently hopeless dejection; some were greatly emaciated, and some, particularly children, seemed dying.*
>
> *But the circumstance which struck us most forcibly was how it was possible for such a number of human beings to exist, packed up and wedged together as tight as they could cram, in low cells three feet high, the greater part of which, except that immediately under the grated hatchways, was shut out from light or air...The space between decks was divided into two compartments 3 feet 3 inches high; the size of one was 16 feet by 18 and of the other 40 by 21; into the first were crammed the women and girls, into the second the men and boys: 226 fellow creatures were thus thrust into one space 288 feet square and 336 into another space 800 feet square, giving to the whole an average of 23 inches and to each of the women not more than 13 inches. We also found manacles and fetters of different kinds, but it appears that they had all been taken off before we boarded.*
>
> *The heat of these horrid places was so great and the odour so offensive that it was quite impossible to enter them, even had there been room. They were measured as above when the slaves had left them. The officers insisted that the poor suffering creatures should be admitted on deck to get air and water. This was opposed by the mate of the slaver, who, from a feeling that they deserved it, declared they would murder them all.*
>
> **Task: The Middle Passage**
>
> **Consider the diagram and Reverend Walsh's account. What do these reveal about conditions on the ships?**
>
> **How are these conditions reflected in Beloved's 'memories'?**

The end of slavery?

Emancipation

Term used to refer to an individual or group freedom.

Beloved opens in 1873 and as such the African-American population of Cincinnati, along with those in other states, should have been enjoying over a decade of freedom and 'reconstruction'. President Abraham Lincoln had signed the Emancipation Act on April 16th of 1860. The act compensated slave holders and offered to pay freed slaves a sum of they chose to leave America and colonize other countries. There was some surprise that most chose to stay.

It was almost two years later when General Robert E Lee surrendered at Appomattox, ending the American Civil War and applying the Emancipation Proclamation to the Southern states. Texas ignored the Proclamation and it took until June 19, 1865 (now known as 'Juneteenth'), when General Granger issued the order at Galveston, Texas, that 'all slaves are free'.

This was not the full independence desired, as freedmen were advised 'to remain quietly at their present homes, and work for wages'. They were expected to remain with former owners and there was no suggestion of compensation for life in slavery.

I was the conductor of the Underground Railroad for eight years, and I can say what most conductors can't say — I never ran my train off the track and I never lost a passenger.

Harriet Tubman, 1896

Harriet Tubman (1823 – 1913)
nurse, spy and scout

The Underground Railroad

The Underground Railroad was a network of people, safe houses and refuges, and communities that were connected by land, rail, and sea routes. It existed through collaboration between abolitionists and slaves, providing escape routes from the brutal conditions forced upon African Americans. The goal was to assist enslaved people in gaining their freedom. Many moved through the north to Canada. Ohio was geographically significant as crossing the Ohio River provided the first step to freedom from the slavery supporting southern states.

The Fugitive Slave Act 1850

It was not enough to make it to safety in Ohio, as Sethe tragically learns. Even in a free northern state, African Americans continued to face the threat of being returned to a slaveholder due to the 1850 Fugitive Slave Act. This act required that all escaped enslaved persons be returned to their masters when captured.

Cartoon illustrating how northern states helped slave owners hunt down escaped slaves.

Source: **Fugitive Slave Act September 1850**

Section 3

And be it further enacted, That the Circuit Courts of the United States shall from time to time enlarge the number of the commissioners, with a view to afford reasonable facilities to reclaim fugitives from labour, and to the prompt discharge of the duties imposed by this act.

Section 4

And be it further enacted, That the commissioners above named shall have concurrent jurisdiction with the judges of the Circuit and District Courts of the United States, in their respective circuits and districts within the several States, and the judges of the Superior Courts of the Territories, severally and collectively, in term-time and vacation; shall grant certificates to such claimants, upon satisfactory proof being made, with authority to take and remove such fugitives from service or labour, under the restrictions herein contained, to the State or Territory from which such persons may have escaped or fled.

Section 6

Claimants and marshals enabled 'to use such reasonable force and restraint as may be necessary, under the circumstances of the case, to take and remove such fugitive person back to the State or Territory whence he or she may have escaped as aforesaid. In no trial or hearing under this act shall the testimony of such alleged fugitive be admitted in evidence; and the certificates in this and the first [fourth] section mentioned, shall be conclusive of the right of the person or persons in whose favour granted, to remove such fugitive to the State or Territory from which he escaped, and shall prevent all molestation of such person or persons by any process issued by any court, judge, magistrate, or other person whomsoever.

Section 7 Right to prosecute anyone harbouring a slave or obstructing marshals or agents.

Section 10 And the said court, commissioner, judge, or other person authorized by this act to grant certificates to claimants or fugitives, shall, upon the production of the record and other evidences aforesaid, grant to such claimant a certificate of his right to take any such person identified and proved to be owing service or labour as aforesaid, which certificate shall authorize such claimant to seize or arrest and transport such person to the State or Territory from which he escaped.

TASK: How does the language used in the act support the dehumanisation of slaves?

Locate the sections of the act where you can find the following:

– **Granting of additional powers to enable escaped slaves to be captured**
–**Grants claimant the right to reclaim slave and return them to service**
– **Prosecution for aiding escaped slaves**
– **Claimants given authority to capture escaped slaves**
– **Allowing use of force and denying the escaped slave the right to testify.**

The Language of Slavery

Abolitionist

An abolitionist takes a political position against the institutional slavery. Most were politically active.

The abolitionist may not always be acting on anti-slavery values when helping individuals to escape.

There are a number of terms relating to slavery that are referenced and alluded to in the novel. It is important to consider the implications of these terms.

In the text, Sethe and others regard Garner and school teacher as *'masters'* and slave *'owners'*, as many slaves were taught at the time. The alternative term *'slave holder'* does not accept that one human being can ever own another. This is a preferred term of the resistance movement, and may be how Garner regarded himself, although Baby Suggs, Paul D and Halle have come to recognise that Garner's good intentions only go some way to alleviate the fact that he has traded in and seen profit from other human beings.

The Bodwins pride themselves on being *abolitionists* and have supported both Baby Suggs and Sethe in establishing a home and employment in Cincinnati. Towards the end of the novel, Morrison has Bodwin reflect on his disappointment with the abolitionist cause in the latter half of the nineteenth century. While politically active, and a practical support with the local Underground Railroad, he nevertheless entertains plantation owners and has Baby Suggs and later Denver restricted to entering his house at the back door.

Similarly, Sethe is regarded as a *fugitive*. Those teaching the history of the Underground Railroad today make important points about those human beings seeking their right to individual freedoms. The word *'fugitive'* has connotations of criminal behaviour and suggests an outlaw, while '*runaway*' suggests a disobedient child. The Railroad was a form of civil disobedience but the term *'freedom seeker'* is now preferred.

Sethe is the ultimate freedom seeker, choosing to kill her children rather than risk them losing their individual freedoms. The term *'slave'* itself suggests an acceptance of the dehumanisation of the system of slavery. '*Enslaved*' is a more useful term which recognises that one human being has been placed in an abject position due to the social and historical constraints of the time.

1.4 Literary Contexts: Slave narratives and the supernatural

In this section we will;
- *Demonstrate understanding of the significance and influence of the contexts in which Beloved was written and received*
- *Explore connections across literary texts and contexts*
- *To consider wider social and historical contexts*

Morrison and the 'Great' Tradition

While Morrison's project has clearly been to present stories of women and black communities there are others who see her work as embracing and drawing on western literary models. There are elements of Morrison's style which reflect the writing of authors like Faulkner and Woolf, particularly in the fragmentation of time in her writing and the use of third person limited narration and free indirect discourse.

Morrison would reject approaches that place all novels in the Western tradition as *'it never goes into the work on its own terms'* (p.122 *Black Women Writers at Work* Ed. Claudia Tate, NY, Continuum. 1984).

Beloved has elements of historical slave narratives, gothic horror and modernist fictions. The novel explores the trauma of slavery as presented in memories and the perpetual hurt of those memories. Memory is used as a metaphorical sign of interior life.

Morrison saw the problems of presenting the interior life when evidence is sparse. She is uncomfortable with labels such as the 'fantastic' and 'magical' when applied to her fiction. She tries to address the gaps in the slave narratives so she can 'part the veil'.

Beloved as 'slave narrative'

Unlike earlier slave narratives, Morrison makes memory dialogic through using several characters to tell the story. She also seeks to challenge the reader's sense of linear time. The novel highlights that women become both the means and source of production. As such, they are under threat from slave catchers who wish to keep them producing and see all children as profit and future slaves.

Sethe murders Beloved to save her from the future, just as she works to shield Denver from the past. Sethe withholds information, from others and herself. Memories bring both consolation and anguish. Sethe's processes of re-memory and disremembering indicate the amount of work put into repressing and forgetting traumatic experiences. Beloved as the 'rebuked' ghost is also repressed.

American slave narratives

Frederick Douglass (1818-1895)

Abolitionist, writer and statesman.

He described his time as a slave in his 1845 *Narrative of the Life of Frederick Douglass, an American Slave.*

This popular text promoted abolition of slavery. He also wrote *My Bondage and My Freedom* (1855) and the *Life And Times of Frederick Douglass* (1881, revised in 1892).

Morrison presented views on slave narratives in her lecture 'The Site of Memory', originally published in *Inventing the Truth: The Art and Craft of Memoir* (1987).

Morrison aims to explore what is said and unsaid in traditional slave narratives. These texts were autobiographical in nature and presented narrative in a linear fashion. Many charted the journey from bondage to freedom, silence to language, ownership to possession, feeling like 'other' to discovery of self.

'You have seen how a man was made a slave; now you shall see how a slave was made a man'

Narrative of the life of Frederick Douglass (1845)

Morrison reminds us that the slave narrative was also a political text. These stories were used to further the abolitionist campaigns in the years leading to the Civil War (1861-1865). While the abolitionists sought to liberate people, they also made sure to censor the narratives. It was felt that if the whole truth was told there would be a risk of not being believed, given the shocking depravity of some of the treatment. Slave narratives were often presented with prefaces written by white sympathisers, intended to authenticate details of the account that followed.

While the narratives were promoted as factual, presentation of the whole truth risked alienating the white middle-class readership, especially references to sexual violence. This experience was common but often felt unsuitable for a female readership, although alluded to in Harriet Jacobs's *'Incidents in the Life of a Slave Girl: Written by Herself'* (1861). A pattern emerged with the narratives that while written signs of freedom, these texts operated within limited representations deemed to be acceptable. Such limitations were not only related to the exclusion of forms of physical oppression but also what Morrison terms the 'interior life'.

Slave narratives often had a focus on institutions as the aim was the abolition of slavery. In her text, Morrison can focus on internal landscape. The novel serves as a cautionary tale. The community needs a healing ritual from trauma.

Some readers and critics have found *Beloved* to be a brutal text, but Morrison felt this was key to illustrate how strong these individuals had to be to survive. She also shows that individuals have aspirations despite constant oppression.

Morrison felt Garner's case illustrated clearly how slavery denied natural family bonds. In the novel some of the women have felt ambivalent towards children produced through rape and forced procreation. Sethe is an exception in that her children were not 'bred' but a product of love. Her absolute love prompts the ultimate sacrifice of killing rather than having them endure debasement.

The narrative is cyclical rather than chronological. Events are gradually revealed through memories. It encompasses a wide time line, from the final decade of the eighteenth century, when Baby Suggs is born, to early Spring 1875, when Beloved is exorcised from the community.

Further Reading: Slave narratives

For an introduction to key fictional and non-fictional slave narratives, it is worth reading the following Guardian Online article:

https://www.theguardian.com/books/2014/jan/10/12-years-slave-uncle-toms-cabin

---

A new audience

Rather than addressing the white readers who formed the audience for traditional slave narratives, the novel confronts black readers with a past that has been repressed or ignored.

The site of memory is also one of terror and trauma. The novel can be seen as an example of Derrida's 'supplement', an addition to something which appears complete yet is essential to it. *Beloved* contributes to the genre of African-American slave narratives as it is able to dwell on graphic violation. The novel also examines how slavery violates and structures the black subject. It sets out to retrieve elements hidden or encrypted in traditional slave narratives.

This is not only a story about a ghost but has its own ghostly presence 'haunting...the gaps and silences of the tradition on which it draws'. Slave narratives provide print origins for black literature. The key aims were to show a personal life that also represents the race and to persuade the reader to support abandonment of slaves. Early accounts such as the 1789 narrative by Equiano set out to change things.

The accounts of the nineteenth century not only looked to address the issue of slavery, but also to compliment the reader's nobility of heart. Slave narratives sold well with general readers. They demonstrated that literacy does provide power. Texts were often subtitled as 'written by him/ her self' and opened with supporting statements from white sympathizers stressing the humanity of the author.

The wider historical context was that the Age of Enlightenment was also the age of scientific racism. Thomas Jefferson, in his *'Notes on the State of Virginia'* argued that the black population never 'uttered a thought above the level of plain narration, never see even an elementary trait or painting or sculpture'.

The slave narratives sought to answer this, although they have often drawn on the style of the sentimental novel, seeking to move quickly away from violence. Texts remained silent about the worst aspects of slavery. Abolitionist Lydia Maria Child suggested Jacobs's story would see *'the veil drawn aside'*. Morrison aimed to rip that veil.

Morrison invites African-American community to judge more negative elements too. Slave narratives had a focus on institutions as the aim was to encourage abolition of slavery as an institution. Morrison's text maintains a focus on the internal landscape.

The novel serves as a cautionary tale. The community needs a healing ritual to rescue from trauma. In the text there is both pleasure and challenge. The reader is reminded '*This is not a story to pass on!*'

Image of Solomon Northup, co-author of *Twelve Years a Slave*

Intertextuality: *Beloved* and Harriet Beecher Stowe's *Uncle Tom's Cabin*

Critical Reading: Lori Askeland (1992)

'Remodelling the Model Home in *Uncle Tom's Cabin* and *Beloved*'

In her essay, Askeland looks at the ways in which domesticity is presented in *Uncle Tom's Cabin*. She reads *Beloved* as a remodelling of *Uncle Tom's Cabin*, a revision of the slave narrative designed 'to avoid the reification of a patriarchal power structure'.

The nineteenth century saw a 'cult of domesticity'. Harriet Beecher Stowe had previously written of the power of order in the creation of a model home. She venerated the housewife as having the 'sacred duties of the family state'. The word 'domain' links to the Latin word '*domus*'. This place would be a symbol of rules, ownership, mastery and power. The northern European word 'house' has roots in '*hus*' and '*huden*', meaning to hide, shelter, conceal or cover.

There are some parallels between the two novels. The locations of Sweet Home and the Shelby plantation are both in Kentucky. Both texts have characters who undertake dramatic actions in response to the Fugitive Slave Act.

HARRIET BEECHER STOWE.

Harriet Beecher Stowe. Author of *Uncle Tom's Cabin*

Morrison sets her story in Cincinnati 1873. The Beechers had lived there from 1832-1849, and Beecher Stowe would have experienced freed slaves there. The mid 1870s saw a slowdown in the housing reform of the North and the 'reconstruction' of patriarchal structures in the South. Both of the novels rework ideologies that dominate the national power structures.

Simon Legree's house charts the fall from spiritualism to materialism. Cassy turns a '*hus*' into a matriarchal '*domus*' which remains in white power. The community provides a safe but temporary shelter. The house is an idealised matriarchal domain. Cassy is seen as mad in murdering son and plotting revenge on Legree.

Tom sees God as 'slaveholder in sky', albeit a benevolent one. George Shelby teaches his slaves to be good Christians and as the story ends patriarchal power has been restored. Stowe's Christianity still serves to privilege the white groups, too much like slavery for a character like Baby Suggs.

In *Beloved*, Sweet Home is presented as an exemplary Victorian home. Mrs Garner is portrayed as a mother figure by Sethe but is revealed to have limited power. She is not left alone in charge of slaves after Garner's death and in trying to intercede for Sethe she provokes instead a severe beating. The males are ultimately in charge.

Like Arthur Shelby, Garner seems humane but his fragile domain disintegrates on his death. Paul D recognises that he has been defined as a man by Garner and only at Sweet Home.

When he arrives at 124, Paul D banishes the ghost just long enough to suggest a community but soon Beloved demands all from Sethe and Denver. Sethe wants a model family and welcomes Beloved in.

Both Stowe and Morrison note that while woman may create domestic domain, the male can invade and threaten. The novel ends with an alternative model, where men and women can share.

Beloved as a Gothic text

Beloved is a memory tyrant. This is a Gothic convention for ghosts. She draws on each character's insecurities. There is a grim irony that 'her tyranny has strong overtones of slavery's patriarchal force' (Askeland, 1992). Beloved eventually restricts Sethe to the house. She drives Sethe and Denver to the point of madness. Beloved takes away her claim, becoming 'the epitome of patriarchal possession' (Askeland,1992).

Denver reaches out and the community confront the possession. When Sethe attacks Bodwin it is an attack on the ghost of patriarchal ownership. Beloved as an embodiment of enslavement can disappear. The novel ends with a hope for a domestic ideal beyond a patriarchy. Paul D offers a relationship which is reciprocal – he will 'lay his story next to hers'.

It could be argued that Morrison drew some influence from earlier Gothic texts such as *Frankenstein* or *Dracula*. Like these traditional Gothic texts, the community's fear of Beloved invokes fears surrounding monstrosity and creation. Beloved can be seen as a variant of the monster or the vampire. In Frankenstein, the monster was created by a human and as such was an allegory for the dangers of excessive knowledge and endeavour within humans, while in Dracula the fear is outside. With Beloved, it is possible to suggest she has been 'created' by Sethe's guilt and Denver's isolation. Yet she is equally an external force, seen by Ella as an 'invasion' from the afterlife. Frankenstein's monster subverts creation, while Dracula subverts death and mortality. Beloved can be seen to embody elements of each of these. She is 'birthed' from the creek and seems to exist outside of time, holding memories of the dead baby and the mothers and girls lost on the slave ships of the Middle Passage.

The Gothic and supernatural in Beloved

If we consider Sedgwick's analysis of the characteristics features of Gothic writing, Beloved can be seen to share a number of features with more traditional Gothic texts:

- Through **setting;** traditional Gothic narratives were often set in Catholic European countries, drawing on superstitions and belief in folklore. Beloved may be set in America, but draws on the superstitions and beliefs inherited from the free community's African ancestors.
- **Oppressive landscapes.** Both Sethe and Paul D note the horror lying just below the surface beauty of Sweet Home. 124 is a claustrophobic and isolated house.
- **Stock characters** such as schoolteacher, a flat character representing the evil tyranny of those in power.
- **Tropes and features** such as characters in a trance or deathlike state, subterranean spaces, burials and 'doubling'. Beloved places both Paul D and Sethe in catatonic states at various points in the story, Paul D recounts traumatic memories relating to his underground cell, while Beloved has memories of being buried or submerged. Beloved becomes a double, inhabiting memories of Sethe's child and Sethe's mother's passage on the slave ship almost simultaneously.
- **Unnatural echoes or silences,** or difficulties in communication. Beloved's memories are conveyed through silences and gaps, as well as broken communication of a childlike spirit. Throughout the narrative, all of the characters struggle to communicate the traumas they have experienced.

TASK: Beloved as Gothic novel

Can you find evidence of each of the Gothic features listed below in the opening four chapters?

- *Gothic settings*
- *Oppressive landscapes*
- *Gothic tropes*
- *Stock characters*
- *Unnatural echoes or silences*

Beloved as Urban Gothic

Beloved may also be seen as an example of Urban Gothic as it concludes with disruptive elements expelled and stable categories of family reaffirmed. The text reflects developments in individual and collective identity. It is the community that conquers the vampiric Beloved. The text presents a spiritual conquest of the uninvited guest.

Traditionally, Gothic texts relied on shared, communal knowledge of the supernatural and accepted superstition and religious belief. This would seem to bear out in the exorcism of Beloved. However, there are individuals such as Lady Jones and Paul D, who do not readily accept that Beloved is the dead child returned. In Urban Gothic there is "no implicit knowledge; everything must be tested and proved". There is an attempt to use empirical methods to address the supernatural, as individuals such as Paul D, Stamp Paid and Ella consider a rational explanation for Beloved's presence. They propose that Beloved is a runaway who has amnesia brought on by trauma. One effect of the competing theories is that the text often affirms the supernatural as it attempts to expel it. At the end of the novel, Beloved has disappeared yet she remains in ghostly footprints, becoming something 'not to pass on'.

Beloved as 'invasion' text

Much of the horror of the text is linked to the idea of an invasion of the domestic setting. The genre of the text can be seen as supernatural or 'uncanny'. Looking at Freud's later definition of uncanny it is worth noting the German term used, *'unheimlich'* which translates 'unhomely'. The undead are beyond the familiar or homely as being simultaneously alive and dead but there is also a sense of the women in the text subverting expectations of the domestic sphere.

TASK: Exploring Wider Contexts

Make sure you have read the novel before attempting this task. Aim to respond to each heading with an extended paragraph, making one essay-style response.

Discuss the presentation of key social and historical contexts in the novel.

Historical Contexts

- ❖ What does the novel tell us about life in Kentucky and Ohio in the later part of the nineteenth century?
- ❖ What is revealed about the institution of slavery?
- ❖ What references are made to the American Civil War?

Cultural Contexts

- ❖ How is 'culture' referenced in the novel?
- ❖ How are knowledge and education presented or treated in the narrative?
- ❖ To what extent does culture influence the social order and individual sensibility?

Gender and Sexuality

- ❖ How are males and females presented in the novel?
- ❖ Are certain behaviours or roles presented as masculine and feminine?
- ❖ Does the text challenge or subvert conventional gender stereotypes?
- ❖ In what ways does gender impact upon experiences within the narrative?

Power

- ❖ What power relationships and power struggles are represented?
- ❖ How is the relationship between social classes and the social hierarchy explored?

Race

- ❖ How is race referenced in the novel?
- ❖ Does the narrative voice challenge or support representations of race?

Religion

- ❖ What part does religion play in the narrative?
- ❖ Are there a range of belief systems presented in the text?

Part Two:
Introducing Critical Approaches

2.1 *Narrative, Structure and Style*

2.2 *Characterisation*

2.3 *Themes and Symbolism*

2.4 *Settings: Crossing Boundaries*

2.5 *The 'Other'*

2.1 Narrative, Structure and Style

In this section we will;

- *Develop informed responses to Beloved, using associated concepts and terminology*
- *Analyse ways in which meanings are shaped in texts*
- *Explore literary texts informed by different interpretations*

Narrative Overview

When responding to *Beloved,* you should consider how the writer's linguistic and literary techniques enhance or develop themes and characterisation, and how they contribute to the overall narrative style.

Intertextuality: Margaret Garner

The novel was inspired by the real case of Margaret Garner, who escaped from Kentucky in 1865 with her husband, in-laws and children. Like Sethe, they too fled to Ohio, but were pursued by their owner and marshals wishing to enforce the Fugitive Slave Act.

Margaret killed her daughter as the search party closed in. Her case was followed closely by the newspapers who labelled her the 'modern Medea'. Supremacists saw her actions as proof of diminished humanity and wished her returned to her owner, as slaves were seen as property. Abolitionists wished to see her tried for murder, as proof she was a person in her own sight.

In the end, after a protracted trial, the judge gave into pressure from marshals, and overturned the local sheriff's jurisdiction. He sent the family back down the river to be sold on to other owners. It is believed that one of her remaining children died on the journey back as the boat capsized.

Synopsis of *Beloved*

Beloved charts the life of Sethe, a black woman, from her time as a slave on the Sweet Home plantation in Kentucky to her life in Cincinnati, Ohio, in 1873. A free woman in the present day, she is forever affected by trauma relating to her time as a slave and the subsequent horrors stemming from her decision to kill her young daughter and her attempt to kill all her children when her new owner 'schoolteacher' tracked her down.

In *Beloved*, Sethe exhibits a steadfast devotion and desire to protect her children. She sent the children ahead to grandmother Baby Suggs before being forced to escape the Kentucky plantation whilst heavily pregnant, as a result of the increasingly sadistic abuses practised by the new master of Sweet Home, referred to as 'schoolteacher'.

Sethe attempts infanticide as Margaret Garner had done, killing her unnamed two-year-old as the search party approach to take her back to Sweet Home. Seeing her act, they deem her insane and grudgingly decide to leave her to her fate. The local sheriff takes her to prison to serve a sentence for the murder. She is released within months.

The novel opens in 1873. Sethe and her teenage daughter Denver are living in 124 Bluestone Road, Cincinnati, Ohio. The house is haunted – Sethe's memories make a link to her dead daughter, named Beloved after the engraving Sethe had inscribed on her tombstone. The full details of Sethe's past and Beloved's death are not yet shared with the reader. Information is presented in a series of flashbacks and digressions conveyed through first-person, third-person limited and third-person omniscient perspective.

While information is limited, the reader learns the community shun the residents at 124. The ghost of 124 is challenged by Paul D. A fellow slave at Sweet Home, he has arrived at Sethe's door and begin to share memories and embarks on a physical relationship with Sethe. Like Sethe, he represses memories, storing them in his 'tobacco tin' of a heart. The house seems calmed, and although Denver is initially resentful of the intrusion and frustrated by her isolation, there is a sense of family as they attend a carnival together. On the return from the joyful event, they come across a dishevelled young woman asleep outside 124. Claiming her name as Beloved, she is taken in and nursed back to health. Paul D and Sethe discuss whether she is a traumatised young woman who has escaped from enslavement to a local white man.

Paul D is suspicious of her motives but meets resistance from both Sethe and Denver, who seem enchanted by the new addition to the family. Beloved's questions and comments suggest knowledge of Sethe and Denver believes she is her deceased sister. At certain points Beloved seems something even more powerful than a supernatural revenant. Her strange cryptic speech and disjointed memories recall the trauma faced by female slaves forcefully removed from African nations and taken by sea to slavery in America. Beloved embodies collective memory of the forgotten.

Beginning to suspect that Beloved is her dead daughter miraculously grown and returned, Sethe tries desperately to atone for her actions while Denver vies for Beloved's attention. Beloved seems jealous of Paul D's relationship with Sethe, and plots to drive him out of the home, before seducing him in the cold house.

Paul D now feels guilt and plans to start a family with Sethe, before Stamp Paid shares a newspaper report with him which reveals Sethe's past. Paul D cannot condone her actions or her reasoning and moves out of 124.

As the women are left alone, 124 becomes a negative space. Sethe's obsession with Beloved keeps her house bound and she soon loses her job at Sawyer's restaurant. Beloved is pregnant and ravenous, while Sethe and Denver are starved. Denver overcomes her fascination for her sister and braces herself to approach the community for help.

When Bodwin comes to collect Denver for work, Sethe rushes at him – confusing him in his hat for the schoolteacher. She is restrained and while the gathering women sing and pray, Beloved is said to disappear. As the novel draws to a close, Paul D has reconciled with the bereft Sethe and he urges her to take his support and start a new stage of her life. There is also hope for Denver who has a future as a teacher.

In keeping with the supernatural elements, the final pages suggest that ghostly traces of Beloved remain and the text encourages readers to both forget yet pay remembrance to the victims of slavery.

Style: Narrative Perspective

The novel is characterised by frequent shifts in narrative perspective. Opening with third person omniscient point of view the reader engages with a narrator who knows all about the house. The shift to third-person limited enables a more intimate exploration of the changing perceptions of Lady Suggs.

The series of chapters presented as first-person narratives of Sethe, Denver and Beloved respectively, culminating in a call and response and blurring of narrative voices, serve to emphasise that this is a novel concerned with collective and communal memory. It is a shared story.

The consecutive chapters presented as Beloved's voice also illustrate the concept of 're-memory'. The first iteration is disjointed and appears to lack structure. It is built on gaps and silences, as Beloved the child tries to process a series of disparate sensations and experiences. The second chapter reflects the voice of a version of Beloved who has mastered language to a degree. She has processed some of these memories – this is a 're-memory' as the narrative begins to take shape. Further complexity is evident in the nature of Beloved's memories. Many are beyond her own history and make reference to slaves travelling on transatlantic routes, indicating that she is a voice for the 'sixty million and more', all the 'beloveds' who have been lost to memory since the beginning of slavery. It is a collective voice.

Key Terms: Narrative perspective

First person: The narrator is conveying events from their own point of view. They may be the protagonist, a peripheral eye witness or may be re-telling an earlier experience.
Focalizer: A character through which the story is told; the story is given from their perspective.
Third person omniscient: Here the narrator knows the thoughts and feelings of all the characters.
Third person limited: The narrator knows the thoughts and feelings of one character.

Narrative methods: *Beloved* as Polyphonic Text

While often presented through third-person omniscient and third-person limited narration, the series of first-person narratives provide immediacy and increase the reader's sense of horror and bewilderment; the absence of a dominant voice denies the reader certainty about the reliability of the account.

Throughout the text, the reliability of the point of view being presented must be evaluated. It could be argued that this makes the text more democratic, as it is not privileging a single viewpoint. In this way *Beloved* could be seen as an example of Bakhtin's polyphonic text.

Bakhtin (1981) Novel as Dialogic or Polyphonic Text

Bakhtin sees language "as essentially dialogic; it takes place in a social context".

For him, any word "is directly, blatantly oriented towards a future answer word". He does not find genre a useful way of responding to literary texts. The insistence of categorising deems a text monologic in world view and ideology, suggesting there is one way to interpret it.

For Bahktin, the novel is a dialogic or polyphonic text. He borrows the term 'polyphonic' from musical analysis and sees it as a useful term for the way in which a novel can allow "a number of diverse voices to interact".

Even when a text makes use of a third person narrator, Bakhtin argues that the use of free indirect speech and an implicit reader "embody awareness of its place in an orchestra of different voices with their varied points of view". There is such an orchestra in Beloved, both in voices and media used.

Dialogic: Text characterized by dialogue, rather than monologic, which provides a single point of view.

> **Critical Viewpoint: Nellie McKay on *Beloved*'s Style**
>
> Nellie Y McKay (1998) praises Morrison's style and *Beloved* in particular:
>
> '*In the many voices and memories in this text, Morrison explores and dramatizes the past and present of African-American history through the myth and folklore of many nations and people...Emptied of the values that mark and specify dimension in a Western tradition. Morrison's narrative now belongs to itself – the text claims its text*'. (McKay, 1998).

The sense of 'Telling' in the novel is characterised by dialect, narrative recursion and suspension of time and place. The extended section of the novel told in the voices of Sethe, Denver and Beloved suggest the story cannot be trusted to an individual discourse.

The voices are distinctive. Sethe employs dialect, although there is evidence of sensory description and a sense of poetry in her accounts. Denver's words relate to kinship and memories. There is repetition in her claim upon her sister – 'She's mine, Beloved. She's mine'. Beloved's entries challenge and disrupt the narrative structure and sense. Beyond the opening of her section there is no punctuation and visual gaps create silences, suggesting time and space are not wholly relevant. In Beloved: A Spiritual, Karla Holloway argues this sets it apart from prose conventions:

As this section reaches its final refrain the identity of the speaker almost seems irrelevant. The voices no longer a discourse. Morrison breaks tradition and dissolves constructs of time, creating a literate yet oral text. This is seen as liberating in style.

2.2 Characterisation

In this section we will;
- *Develop informed responses to Beloved, using associated concepts and terminology*
- *Analyse ways in which meanings are shaped in texts*
- *Explore literary texts informed by different interpretations*

Exploring the character of Beloved

Beloved is believed to be the spirit of the unnamed murdered child and 'something more', a collective spirit. Sethe's mother came from Africa so in some way Beloved serves as Sethe's daughter but also the spirit of her mother. She is a liminal character, on the boundary between the living and the dead. Beloved is also a compulsion or force. She compels others to act in certain ways.

Beloved is a symbol of the past and must be confronted as the novel's antagonist. She is 'the return of the repressed'. The family becomes a site to explore time, self and the Other. Beloved is the past, Sethe the present, and Denver the hope for the future.

Beloved as trickster is a deconstructive force. She is irrational like the trickster. There are role reversals of the master/ slave relationship. She ultimately heals although in many ways she causes disruption. Sixo is also a trickster figure in his use of number rather than name and his heroism in death. Tricksters enable psychological healing. Sethe begins to heal when she recognises Beloved. The image of the treasure chest connects wealth and death, both a casket and grave for memories.

Beloved is not just Sethe's ghost, as evidenced in Ella's final decision to help 124. Women create a beginning without words purging Beloved while baptising Sethe back into the community

Beloved serves to recall the other traumas and violations that have been experiences by local women. She takes the reader further back to the conditions on the passage of the slave ships. Beloved is collective memory and so it takes a community of women to exorcise her.

Liminality

Characteristics relating to being in transition, or occupying a position on, or at both sides of, a boundary or significant threshold. Beloved occupies a space between the human and supernatural.

Exploring the character of Sethe

Sethe is an ambiguous maternal figure, although she is the protagonist and emotional centre of the novel. Her own mother had kept her yet Sethe has ambivalent feelings when discovering that her mother was hung while trying to escape without her. Her grief is tempered with abandonment.

Sethe battles to keep her own children – ironically creating the ghost that drives Howard and Buglar away. Sethe sees killing as an act of love.

The name Seth means 'granted' or 'appointed'. In the Bible, Seth was the third child born to replace Abel. In *Beloved,* Sethe is granted parents who loved each other and is the only child kept by her mother, and in turn she will have children through a love match. She may also believe herself appointed to save her child from slavery.

Later in the novel, Ella reflects on her difficulty with Sethe, noting she resents Sethe's lack of acceptance of help. Paul D equally warns Sethe to 'love small'. Sethe has reclaimed the freedom to love. She argues her actions have put her children beyond the harm of white oppressors. The central difficulty is whether this act of love crossed into an act of hate.

History is a form of maternity here, as understanding comes from inside rather than outside forces, challenging the paternalistic models of the past. In telling Beloved her stories, Sethe gains a sense of self. There is an intertextual allusion to *The Scarlet Letter* in Sethe's scar. As with Hester's letter A for Adulteress, both brands are repurposed as identifying and individual markers. History becomes herstory.

There are challenges to the claims for self. The first presentation of Beloved's death is not given by Sethe but given through the collective white, male perspective of the slavecatchers. Schoolteacher and the sheriff see this event as confirming that Sethe is no more than a creature. Stamp Paid seems to accept the newspaper's version of events and Paul D would seem to support this view when he warns *'You got two feet, Sethe, not four'* (*Beloved*, 165).

Sethe fights the characteristics imposed on her. She refutes accusations on wildness. Animality and destructiveness. She remembers her actions as being driven by 'motherhood, motherlines and mother-love'.

The exorcism of Beloved becomes a re-enactment. In going for Bodwin, Sethe now attacks 'the Other' rather than her child. It remains ambiguous whether the deed can ever be defended. The question remains whether grace and redemption are achieved through Beloved or through the removal of Beloved. The text 'neither condemns or condones'.

The novel charts both possession and remembering, and exorcism and forgetting. Mediation between the two states is best. Morrison would seem to suggest that by paying a debt to memory and the past it can be put to rest. The final ambiguity of the tale which is 'not to be passed on' suggests that they must forget yet also not forget.

Exploring the character of Denver

Denver could be argued to be the only character who has true growth. She represents hope for future generations. She has survived exceptional hardships, including her own birth and Sethe's attempt to kill her. Denver has intelligence yet is ruined by the knowledge of Sethe's sin. Denver lacks community.

Like Beloved, Denver is childlike, as when she is truculent with Paul D or her insistence on only hearing her own story. It can be argued that Sethe's attachment to the past has also stymied Denver's growth. At first, Beloved is someone to love. As she matures, Denver realises that Beloved is draining resources and it is Denver is the one who rescues the family.

Denver aims to become a school teacher. She will tell the stories of the past. Denver will continue the struggle with the dual inheritance of freedom and slavery. In the past, Denver could not cope with the references to prison. Sethe has worked hard to hide the past from her. She initially was jealous of the past but her love for Beloved forces her to confront the past and move on. Denver needed history to understand her place.

Exploring the character of Baby Suggs

Although dead at the point when the story begins, stories and memories reveal how Baby Suggs has been the matriarch and guide to Sethe and Denver. She nurtures all and encourages awareness of body and self.

Baby Suggs's generosity is eventually spurned by the community as too much good fortune, just as Paul D struggles with Sethe's claim for love of her family. It is seen as too much. Both Sethe and Baby Suggs in their own ways claim ownership of self. This is taken by the community as pride.

The community are not willing to accept Baby Suggs and her message of loving freely. The community shun Baby Suggs after her party. There are murmured suggestions that she has not suffered as much as others and therefore does not deserve her seeming good fortune. They reject what they perceive as excess. Baby Suggs realises that she never had domain. White men can enter her home. Her freedom is an illusion.

After the community turning their back on 124, Baby Suggs loses faith. She becomes introspective. Baby Suggs and Sethe withdraw from the social community. While she can speak harsh truths, Baby Suggs is often a comforting presence, even after her death. Her 'voice' propels Denver back into the community.

Baby Suggs as Stationmaster

In the mid-century, Baby Suggs also served as a 'Stationmaster', with 124 being an important waystation for those who escaped slavery and then those emancipated but seeking freedom. She provided food, a degree of shelter and information, allowing messages to be left.   This is in sharp contrast to the reclusive woman who withdraws from the harms of society.

Exploring the character of Paul D

Paul D shares horrific memories of slavery and life as a fugitive. He has retained some ability to hope for the future. He comes to 124 and offers an alternative.

This shared past gives Sethe the courage to share memories. Paul D perceives the danger and threat posed by Beloved. Her arrival seems to thwart Sethe's hopes and aspirations. Paul D challenges Sethe to see the truth. He feels bested by Beloved, and leaves when he discovers the truth about Sethe's actions. The revelations are too much to bear.

Paul D initially feels powerless. He is eventually encouraged by Stamp Paid to return to Sethe. He is able to offer to share Sethe's pain and make a new start.

TASK: Paul D

What is your first impression of Paul D?

On reuniting with Sethe, what do his first actions and words reveal about his character?

Remember to select relevant textual examples to support your views.

Stamp Paid

Just as Baby Suggs served as a station master, Stamp Paid often worked as a conductor, guiding people across the river from Kentucky to Ohio, from slavery to freedom. It is for this reason that he expects every door in the area to be open to him and feels spurned by Sethe, while acknowledging that he shares responsibility with the community for exiling Sethe and isolating Denver.

Stamp Paid has a pivotal role in the narrative, playing a vital part in Sethe's escape from Sweet Home, transporting her across the Ohio River, and later sharing information about Sethe's crime with Paul D. He reflects on his own neglect of Sethe and Denver. Later in the novel, he also asks members of the community such as Ella to reflect on their responsibility to others and conveys anger that there has been little support or charity shown towards Paul D.

There will be further discussion of the significance of Stamp Paid's name in 'The Importance of Naming' in Section 4.

Halle

Halle is Sethe's husband and father of all of her children. He is also the son of Baby Suggs. When the novel opens, he is missing, presumed dead, having failed to have followed Sethe in her escape from Sweet Home. Sethe reveals great care for him, but does regard him as a brother as much as a husband.

At the start of the text Sethe has harboured some resentment towards Halle, as she feels he has failed his family in his absence. Paul D reveals that his last sighting of Halle was of him sitting by the churn covered in buttermilk, suggested that he had lost his mind having witnessed Sethe being assaulted by schoolteacher's nephews.

In some memories of Halle, Sethe has revealed that he has an understanding of the restrictions of slavery. While he has worked to raise money to buy his mother's freedom, he is not naïve, and is well aware that in return Sweet Home will seek to claim his wife and children as slaves for decades.

Sixo

Sixo is held up as a model of resistance to slavery. While he does not manage to escape, he does foster a relationship with the Thirty Mile Woman, a young girl who fathers the child that he joyfully christens 'Seven-O!' as the owners burn him to death for his rebellion.

In many of Paul D's memories, he notes Sixo's resistance through his refusal to speak and engage with owners. He shows kindness to his fellow slaves in cooking them potatoes and poaching game to supplement the meagre diet supplied on the plantation. When he does speak it is to challenge schoolteacher's removal of guns from the male slaves.

He is portrayed as something of a trickster or shaman, living on his wits and going to his death with pride. Paul D regards him as an example of real masculinity.

Schoolteacher

He is a detached symbol of evil. His role as a teacher and desire to share his 'knowledge' with the nephews disturbs the reader. In his use of ink and ledgers to record the perceived differences he sees in the slaves he represents the various attempts by supremacists to rationalise racism. There was a belief that other humans were no better than animals. This demonstrates the dangers of dehumanisation. He is a flat rather than a round character.

The Garners

Mr Garner would regard himself as a benign slave holder. He regards his slaves as men and encourages them to express their views. On the plantation they are allowed to bear arms, and Sethe and Halle are recognised as a family unit along with their children.

While Garner seems to be somewhat progressive, and Mrs Garner shows some kindnesses, such as the gift of earrings given to Sethe, the fact remains they are southern slave holders whose wealth has been built on the work of humans they regard as their property. Sethe glosses some more problematic aspects, such as Paul D's brother- also named Paul – being sold to recoup debts owing on the farm and Garner dismissing Baby Suggs's name, preferring to call her by her slave name, Jenny Whitlow. Halle also points out that he paid a large sum to Garner to save his mother from potentially dying on the job, and in return the children would possibly remain at Sweet Home in debt across generations.

The Bodwins

The Bodwins are minor characters who nevertheless provide an interesting portrait of abolitionists. On one hand they are well-meaning and do provide practical help and support for those settling in Cincinnati, providing Baby Suggs with a home and all three generations of women with employment. However, they also demand much from their paid 'free' servants and segregate black maids and workers to the back door while entertaining plantation owners in the main living room.

Lady Jones

Lady Jones is something of a positive force in that she provides education and literacy for the local children, and plays an important part in reintegrating Denver into the community. However, Morrison does convey a degree of complexity in this minor character. Lady Jones is of mixed heritage, a product of miscegenation and forced sexual relations between slaves and master. As such, she is treated with suspicion and is shunned by both black and white communities. She hates her pale colouring and hair and has not accepted herself. Like Sethe she is somewhat outside the community. When the women gather to exorcise Beloved at the end of the novel, she refuses to partake it what she regards as backwards superstition.

Ella

Ella leads the thirty women to banish Beloved and prevent the invasion of the community. She has a history of shared experiences with others. As assumed of Beloved on her appearance, Ella has suffered a past trauma. She was held by a white father and son and repeatedly raped. She can be regarded as the antithesis of Sethe. Ella has actively set out to destroy the children produced while held hostage by the evil white men. Unlike Sethe, Ella's actions were driven by repulsion rather than love. It may be for this reason that she felt both Sethe and Baby Suggs were granted 'too much' in life.

Ella is not a selfish woman, and despite her own difficulties, has played an active part in the Underground Railroad, supporting Stamp Paid and Baby Suggs in escorting many men and women to freedom. However, her mistrust of Sethe has tempered her charity, and she had refused to help Paul D until Stamp Paid shamed her into recognising her own prejudices. While she cannot wholly empathise with Sethe, her belief in community prompts her to act and gather a group to save Sethe from Beloved.

TASK: Minor Characters

What is the significance of Lady Jones, Ella and Bodwin to the larger narrative?

You should consider:

- Aspects of language and imagery relating to each character
- Links to larger themes

CORBIN'S BODY WAS DRAGGED TO A TREE IN THE PARK.

Newspaper sketch of a lynching

EXAM-STYLE RESPONSE: Men in the Novel

In Beloved, Morrison explores the ways in which men were emasculated by slavery.

With reference to Morrison's narrative methods, and relevant contextual information, show to what extent you agree with the above statement.

2.3 Themes and Symbolism

In this section we will;
- *Develop informed responses to Beloved, using associated concepts and terminology*
- *Analyse ways in which meanings are shaped in texts*
- *Explore literary texts informed by different interpretations*

Home

The first thing the reader is told is that '*124 was spiteful. Full of a baby's venom*' (Chapter 1). This house is not a home. Denver's brothers have abandoned '*the lively spite the house felt for them*' (Chapter 1). There is no point in Sethe moving to escape the ghost as there is '*not a house in the country ain't packed to its rafters with some dead Negro's grief*' (Chapter 1).

Paul D feels security in his relationship with Sethe but is restricted by the house: '*He believed he was having house-fits, the glassy anger men sometimes feel when a woman's house begins to bind them...*'

He cannot explain his unrest, as it is not related to his feelings for Sethe; '*In the house fit there was no anger, no suffocation, no yearning to be elsewhere*' (Chapter 11).

Sethe's memories of Sweet Home are idealised. She began work there as a young girl, and she does recall happy times with Halle as well as the abuse that followed. Halle and Paul D are more circumspect and while they valued some of the leniency shown Paul D has learnt the bitter truth that '*...they were only Sweet Home men at Sweet Home*' (Chapter 13).

Baby Suggs also came to this conclusion in her time with the Garners. As she reflects on her experiences, she repeats that she works in '*Lilian Garner's house*' and recognises '*It's better here, but I'm not*' (Chapter 15).

There is irony in the fact that Sethe learns the true value of home and comfort at a time when Beloved has sabotaged her attempts at constructing a new family unit with Denver and Paul D. In Chapter 19, Sethe locks the door so '*...the women inside were free at last to be what they liked, see whatever they saw and say whatever was on their minds*'.

124 has the potential to be a homestead. The house and land were owned by Bodwin, with property stretching to 80 acres on both sides. Bodwin appreciated having tenants to keep the house from abandonment; '*There was a time when he buried things there. Precious things he wanted to protect*' (Chapter 26).

Men and Masculinity

TASK: Masculinity and Community

Men need to be 'claimed' for a meaningful life.

Examine the interactions between Paul D and Stamp Paid. Consider the attitudes towards masculinity presented in their conversations.

Garner may praise his slaves as '*men*' but still brags, calling them '*niggers*' and trying to establish himself as tough. All the male slaves in Sweet Home were there '*waiting for the new girl' (Chapter 1)*.

Halle is a son, a husband and an absent friend. Others '*claim his absence for themselves*', although Denver does not feel able to claim her father.

Paul D remembers Sixo. Paul D regards Sixo as a real man due to his resistance to authority. In the second chapter he reflects '*now there was a man, and that was a tree*' (Chapter 2). This tree means more to him than the 'tree' on Sethe's back after their first disappointing sexual encounter.

Sethe respects her missing husband Halle but does recall that it was not a passionate relationship: '*Halle was more like a brother than a husband*'. Baby Suggs does not trust men, but does value family; '*But a son? Well now, that's somebody*' (Chapter 2).

Paul D feels emasculated by Beloved. In Chapter 3 he recalls staying in a well, and watching a man burn but he cannot face or counter her powers.

Paul D remembers the importance of being able to trust men that you suffer alongside. On the chain gang '*A man could risk his own life, but not his brother's* (Chapter 10). In chapter 13, he does praise Garner's approach – '*they were believed and trusted, but most of all they were listened to*' (Chapter 13)

Naming

Naming is also critical to the construction of self. It is a way of asserting self and removing from nothing. The verb 'called' links to the epigraph from the Bible, and suggests a reclaiming of self. Beloved herself is more ambiguous. She has a liminal existence. She confronts the violent past but also reveals the disabling stasis of the present. The text is filled with references to living and dying.

Time and the construction of memory

It may be useful to consider 'aspect' rather than reference time in the novel. Our normal conception of time limits understanding to think of past, present and future in a linear fashion. The traditional Western construct of time does not define (re)memory.

The concept of re-memory is one of suspension; 'Living itself is suspended in this story because of the simultaneous presence of the past' (Holloway). This is evident in other works by Morrison such as *Sula*, where the protagonist comments on her own death, and *Song of Solomon*, where Circe defies time.

Rather than the passing of time used to mark chronology in a narrative, here sections begin with marked changes in the house. This reflects the idea that the narrative concerns are conceptual rather than temporal.

The challenge for Sethe throughout the novel is to find a way of organising and processing her memories. She needs to shape her own narrative. She 'must learn to represent the unspeakable and unspoken in language' (Holloway).

That 'Beloved' is an inscription often found on a tombstone suggests the haunting in the text. Yet it is also an affectionate term, whilst retaining echoes of a eulogy and the marriage service. These are linguistic events and in the novel Beloved also forces Sethe to place memories into words.

In some senses the novel is resolutely in the present struggling with an unresolved past and reluctant to face or anticipate the future.

History and Memory

Sethe's scars diminish her and mark her as property. Her site of scars serves as a memory trace. The women interpret the horror with natural images, Amy Denver's 'chokecherry tree' and Baby Suggs converting the horrific bleeding to blooming roses on Sethe's back. Paul D sees first a maze and then compares to twisted metal. Sethe can only see herself and her scars through the eyes of others. Her back is numb and likewise her mind is numb as she is unable to feel memories.

Extreme violence silences women, as when Baby Suggs tends to Sethe's wounds 'wordlessly' and later abandons preaching to take to her bed following Sethe's attempt to kill all her children.

In opposition to this, schoolteacher sees himself as a cultural historian and takes it upon himself to write the history of Sethe. He decides to measure the degree of humanity, seeking to reinforce the 'otherness' of the black slaves. He casts them as savage animals in opposition to his civility and humanity. He creates an opposition of culture and nature. He demeans the slaves at Sweet Home, as when Paul D overhears a calculation of 'his worth'. Throughout the text, schoolteacher engages in dismemberment of slaves, physically and mentally. In a further violation he condones the taking of Sethe's milk, stealing from her future as this is the nourishment for her baby.

As Sethe gradually confronts her memories of Sweet Home and the death of Beloved, history frees her. Beloved acts as a return of the past, providing Sethe with a mirror.

Beloved embodies the past. This is the true vampire or succubus draining life from the living. However, to forget or dismiss the past is to forget or disavow slavery. There is a need for collective memory.

Sethe stresses the importance and force of what she terms 're-memory'. This non-standard term, along with the fear of 'disremembering', emphasises the real physical impact caused by returning to past trauma. For Sethe, re-memory is something that she cannot control. Images and experiences return to her suddenly and sap her strength. Later in the text, she can appreciate re-memory as a way of constructing and making sense of past experiences. The converse term 'disremembering' is stronger than the process of forgetting or repressing as it seems to disintegrate the self as well.

Beloved's memories seem to go beyond a single person and reach into the past long before the death of Sethe's daughter. She embodies a collective memory of the injustices served to women in the process of capturing, transporting and enslaving human beings.

It can be argued that the past is the story. As Paul D and Sethe exchange memories we get both history and 'her story'; the modern reader is provided with horrific and graphic details of life before and after slavery.

Memory is used as a metaphorical sign of the interior life. Unlike earlier slave narratives Morrison makes memory dialogic. The text presents challenges to linear time. Sethe murders Beloved to save her from the future; she fights to protect Denver from the past. Memories bring both consolation and anguish, as in the gravestone with the bartered inscription. The vernacular terms of re-memory and disremembering show this is a daily struggle as Sethe works hard to forget. The ghost is rebuked, which has an older meaning of repressed.

Slavery

The text desires a re-visioning of slavery. Sethe represents those who need to undertake a cognitive reclamation of shared spiritual history. Morrison had presented a critical response to nineteenth century slave narratives in her own theoretical work. She felt that these slaves wrote thoughtfully but were forced to omit 'things too terrible to relate'. These things usually involved sexual exploitation or extreme cases of violence and degradation. Morrison aims 'to part the veil', but in this case for black society rather than the white abolitionists who were the intended primary audience for the original slave narratives.

There was a degree of hegemony in the mostly male slave narratives placed alongside the 'master' narratives of mainstream fiction. *Beloved* writes back and challenges both, highlighting the 'disremembered' and unaccounted for lives.

The Fugitive Slave Act was a punitive piece of legislation which prolonged the suffering of those who naively hoped to be free from the tyranny of slavery in unionist states.

Mr Garner is presented as a mainly benign presence who does not fit the typical model of a slave master. From the outset, Garner sees his slaves as superior. He taunts other plantation owners stating *'Y'al got boys'*. He declares proudly that on Sweet Home his slaves are *'men every one'* (Chapter 1).

Paul D perhaps does not share this view. He reveals how dehumanising slavery can be when he confesses to jealousy towards the rooster – pertinently named Mister. Paul D tries to articulate the nature of his jealousy;

'He looked so...free. Better than me. Stronger, tougher...he was still king and I was.... Paul D cannot bear his lack of agency. The lack of freedom is destructive while *'Mister was allowed to be and stay what he was'* (Chapter 12).

Paul D encounters further traumas including the threat of sexual assault and degradation on the Georgia chain gang, alongside the terror of almost being buried alive in the underground cells. He had felt some benefit under Garner's care and appreciated that he did not fear his slaves' opinions. Garner gave the men some sense of self while schoolteacher *'taught them otherwise'*.

Schoolteacher's lesson was *'A truth that waved like a scarecrow in rye; they were only Sweet Home men at Sweet Home'* (Chapter 13).

Baby Suggs in her own reflections is cynical about the motivations of white people, suggesting that Bodwins help *'because they hated slavery worse than they hated slaves'*. Baby Suggs sees dangers in Garner's attempt at 'benign' slavery. She also dehumanises males when she fears *'the dangers of men-bred slaves on the loose'*.

Critics who are not African-American often frame responses to the novel by stating the limitations of any response from a particular position of privilege. The direct impact of slavery and enduring aspects of its legacy cannot truly be understood in these terms. The novel does seek to provide a collective memory and stimulate reflection on the ways in which not only experiences of cruelty but the efforts of a whole community to repress difficult aspects of history can harm future generations, as seen in Denver's isolation and fear of community at the start of the novel. There is hope, as seen in the concluding pages when Paul D offers to put his 'story' next to Sethe's, and Denver has re-entered the community, with aspirations to teach and developing feelings for Nelson Lord.

There is an interesting shift in perspective when the first explicit description of Beloved's murder is conveyed through the eyes of schoolteacher. As a slave holder, he essentially expresses disgust at spoiled property;

'there was nothing left to claim...now she'd gone wild' (Chapter 16).

He again sees this as a teaching moment, hoping his nephew would *'see what happened when you overbeat creatures God had given you the responsibility of – the trouble it was, and the loss'* (Chapter 16).

Bodwin would seem to validate Baby Suggs's cynicism when he reflects on his time as an abolitionist on his way to collect Denver from 124. He learnt his anti-slavery position from his father, who taught him *'human life is holy, all of it'* (Chapter 26). In his later life *'he had less and less reason to believe it'*. He misses the 'old days' of campaigning, and doesn't seem motivated to fight for the rights of freed slaves.

Love

Sethe's love is described as *'too thick'* (Chapter 18). It is possessive and in turn she is possessed by her memories and regrets.

All three women make claims on each other with each declaring *'she is mine'*. Beloved at times has a child's desire for acceptance as she seeks a smile from her absent mother. Psychologically the smile is the social bond between parent and child that Beloved has not experienced. At the end of the text there is a moment of acceptance as they release each other – Beloved can forgive as her mother now defends her from the outsider crossing the yard, Sethe can recognise there were ways to defend her children which did not result in death.

Some critics have considered the ways in which the text presents the three Greek concepts of love – *agape, eros* and *philia*. Paul D and Sethe are brought together through *eros* or impulsive physical desire, while her relationship with Halle seems to embody *philia*, as she regards him as a brother as much as a husband. Later Beloved will compel Paul D to have sex with her while his relationship with Sethe becomes filial. Denver and Beloved share the love of siblings. The purest love is *agape*. Strictly defined as man's love for god, here it represents the later seventeenth century idea of communal or charitable feeling. This is what is missing at the opening of the narrative and what is required to remove Beloved from 124.

The baby casts a powerful spell; although Sethe counters it is *'No more powerful than the way I loved her'* (Chapter 1). The baby dies unnamed, gaining the name Beloved only when Sethe sets out to mark her grave. Denver seems starved of love and in turn hungers for Beloved's attentions, *'looking was food enough to last'* (Chapter 12).

Later in the text, Paul S calls Sethe's love 'too thick' and is angry to think 'that bitch' Beloved is above them, listening to their argument. Paul D sees 124 as a dysfunctional family.

However, Sethe has a binary vision of love; *'Love is or it ain't. Thin love ain't love at all'* (Chapter 18). It can be natural and epic, as Stamp Paid reflects that Baby Suggs was *'the mountain to his sky'* (Chapter 19).

Beloved tries to express her love in the language of a young child;

'Sethe sees me see her and I see the smile...now we can join'. (Chapter 22).

In the next chapter Beloved, Sethe and Denver joining a chorus of claiming and possessing love;

> *'I waited for you*
> *You are mine*
> *You are mine*
> *You are mine' (Chapter 23).*

There is a more equitable and positive image of love when Sixo tries to explain his love for the Thirty Mile Woman; *'The pieces I am, she gather them and give them back to me in all the right order'*. He counsels Paul D to seek *'a woman who is a friend of your mind'*. At the end of the novel Paul D encourages Sethe to value herself as an individual as well as a mother – *'You your best thing Sethe. You are' (Chapter 27)*. They will try to repair themselves together.

There is a small irony that in a text urging remembrance of the forgotten, Beloved must be banished and cast out of the community and her corporeal form;

> *'Although she has claim, she is not claimed...'. As the novel draws to a close the environment seems to 'swallow her all away'* (Chapter 28).

Family

The text is marked by broken and dysfunctional families. The idea of family has been corrupted by the commodification of human beings in the institution of slavery. When people are treated as property, women are mainly valued for their ability to produce more property and profit for the owner, and children are seen as a way to increase profit and sustain labour over generations. Many of the women have been violated and raped in order to produce more bodies to work. On some plantations, slaves have been forced together to produce children, regarded as 'chattel' or property. The women often reject these children as they cannot bond with them. Baby Suggs and Ella recall the trauma of lost children.

Sethe is an exception to this pattern. Sethe was shown respect by the male slaves and was able to make a love match with Halle. She does regard him as a platonic rather than romantic love, describing him *'like a brother'* (Chapter 2). All of her children are with her husband and she is willing to defend the integrity of her family – which she regards as '*my best thing'* – using every measure available to her. She will sacrifice all to protect her family. There is a feeling that even though she has the rare pleasure of an intact family but seems to want more.

This type of love is seen as excessive and it could be argued that it has served to break up the family. The boys have left home and Denver has become isolated from the wider community. Paul D arrives and offers some sense of interaction. Sethe is quick to push him away when he challenges Denver's behaviour and Beloved's motivations;

'*Grown don't mean nothing to a mother. A child is a child'* (Chapter 4).

Denver may be in young adulthood but for Sethe '*In my heart it don't mean a thing'* (Chapter 4). Her children will be protected forever.

It can be argued that in *Beloved* family is not necessarily relations. Baby Suggs is Halle's mother but offers her heart and home to Sethe. Beloved's relation to Sethe and Denver is ambiguous. She may be the deceased baby returned or she may be a lost runaway.

At the carnival, Paul D seeks to reintegrate them with community and help them enjoy themselves:

'*Sethe returns the smiles she got. Denver was swaying with delight. And on the way home, although leading them now, the shadows of three people still held hands'* (Chapter 4).

This is the first time venturing from the house in a social capacity and is a cause for hope. It is at this moment Beloved appears, disrupting the new family grouping.

Sethe never knew her own mother; '*She must of nursed me two or three weeks – that's the way the others did. Then she went back to rice and I sucked from another woman whose job it was*' (Chapter 6). One memory is of her mother taking her behind the smokehouse to show her the mark on her rib, a way of knowing '*This is your ma'am. This*'. It is a way of knowing her body. Sethe in her innocence asks for a mark too and is slapped for it.

The nursemaid Nan tells Sethe how special she was to her mother as a child born out of love. Ma'am had rejected children born as a result of rape and abuse; '*She threw them all away but you...I am telling you small girl Sethe*' (Chapter 6).

Later in the novel Baby Suggs recalls her own children and how she lost them through slavery or death; she mourns '*fingers she never saw become the male or female hands a mother could recognise anywhere*' (Chapter 15). She mourns the fact '*All seven were gone or dead – then came Halle*'. She comments on the whim of her owners; '*But for some reason they let her keep him. He was with her everywhere*' (Chapter 15).

This indicates that Baby Suggs had the capacity to love deeply and it was taken from her numerous times. Her case was not exceptional and serves to highlight the abuse and deep psychological trauma created through this inhumane society.

Sethe's love is presented as being almost primal. She explains that if Beloved's siblings had not survived the attempt on their lives, she would have happily killed herself to reunite with her daughter – '*my mind was homeless then*'. Home and family are constantly related. Sethe feels at home now that Beloved has returned. There is an irony in that the revenant Beloved embodies the uncanny.

The Supernatural and uncanny

Throughout the text the past makes itself known through supernatural presences, from the poltergeist and venomous atmosphere of 124 to the mysterious appearance of Beloved, who emerges from the river.

It is significant that Beloved appears at the exact moment when Sethe entertains a slim hope of constructing a romantic life with Paul D, and building a new family for Denver.

It can also be argued that Beloved serves as a form of trickster. She appears because Sethe refuses to let go of the past.

---

he 'Uncanny' in *Beloved*

antasy is both a literary genre and a term from Freudian psychology. Elements of the text draw on the oncept of the uncanny.

ndrew Bennett and Nicholas Royle explain the uncanny as relating 'specifically with a disturbance of the amiliar'. The concept of the 'uncanny' was drawn from Freud's essay Das Unheimliche (The uncanny or inhomely') and links to ideas of repression.

i Freud's discussion he noted that the word for 'uncanny' was also the word for 'unhomely'. The second et of meanings for heimlich or homely equates to something concealed or hidden from others. Grimm's ictionary of 1877 also suggests that belonging to the home is also those things which can be concealed om strangers. The translation perhaps loses some of this nuance and ambiguity but it remains that home an be a place of secrets as well as a place of comfort and security. This ambiguity underpins Freud's eading of relationships - the uncanny is not new or alien but something familiar which is alienated or hanged through repression.

Community

Throughout the novel there is a sense that individuals need to feel part of a community to help survival. Baby Suggs builds a religious community beyond the constraints of organised faith groups. She urges others to join in a celebration of the body and the self.

Sethe is exiled from the community of the townspeople after the murder. This isolation not only has a negative impact on Denver and the sons who have left home, but also enables Sethe to deny her past and repress memories in a way which prevents her from moving forward and learning to accept herself.

The isolation of Sethe has served a function for the community. Communities often need an outcast to function and reinforce codes of behaviour. Sethe initially may provide an example of a scapegoat. If a moral crime can be seen as the responsibility of a socially marginalised person or group of people, purification can be achieved through exile or killing. The community will be cleansed. In the novel, Sethe is the original scapegoat, but is replaced by Beloved who has invaded the space of the living. Community is restored when the women work together to remove Beloved from 124.

Task: Thematic Concerns

There is no real community in Beloved.

To what extent can this perspective be supported by the events in the novel?

Scapegoating

Key term: psychomachia

The eternal struggle between good and evil. Literally, the 'battle for the soul'.

Anthropologists such as Mary Douglass have noted that pollution fears and accusations of witchcraft share characteristics across place and time. The use of the idiom 'witch-hunt' draws on this. Society seeks to view the universe as dualistic. Clear boundaries separate a group from danger of foreignness. Simplistic notions of purity inside a group against the evil outside are promoted to maintain group identity and security. Northop Frye notes the concept of *psychomachia* - the eternal struggle between good and evil where evil is defeated.

Scapegoating draws on a model of outsider pollution. There were pressures to conform while the model was losing its clarity. The struggle to maintain power can create scapegoats. Whole social groups such as the Jewish community can be used as scapegoats for social problems. Women were also the target of moral campaigns.

It is useful to look at scape-goating or the use of ritual victim in *Beloved*. Beloved has to be sacrificed to restore lost order. The scapegoat should be of the community, although marginal. Initially, Beloved does not seem to fit this definition. She is young, beautiful and mysterious. However, it can be argued that her social links are tenuous. She cannot remember family or connections. This places her as an outsider. As with Gothic scapegoats such as Lucy in *Dracula*, Beloved possesses a flawed rather than controlled sexuality. Paul D is unsettled by her 'shining' appearance. However, unlike traditional scapegoats she has power and makes others yield to her and seems to place both Paul D and Sethe in a trance.

This power suggests the alternative possibility of Sethe as a scapegoat. She lives on the periphery of the community of Cincinnati. She has been regarded as too proud and has been polluted by her act of violence. By ostracizing Sethe the other women can separate themselves from their own mistakes.

The text concludes with the realisation that the community must confront Beloved together. This acts as a communal purification. The exorcism takes on the characteristics of a religious ritual although it is built on older traditions.

ASK: Examination Style Response

Beloved is a novel about the victory of good over evil.

With reference to Morrison's narrative methods, and relevant contextual information, show to what extent you agree with the above statement.

You can consider Beloved as scapegoat within this response.

Image of freed family

2.4 Setting – Crossing Boundaries

In this section we will;
- *Develop informed responses to Beloved, using associated concepts and terminology*
- *Analyse ways in which meanings are shaped in texts*
- *Explore literary texts informed by different interpretations*

Whole Text Analysis: Settings

Analysis of settings requires the reader to consider the places described and how these may relate to the themes of the novel.

LEAP OF THE FUGITIVE SLAVE.

Cincinnati and the Ohio river

Ohio presents a cultural dichotomy. It is a free state. Northern territories including the state of Ohio were said to be safe areas supporting the abolition of slavery. The Ohio River was seen as a modern equivalent to the River Jordan, carrying slaves who had escaped the southern plantations to liberation.

Cincinnati is home to a black population who are deemed free while to the south lies Kentucky, with risks of lynching and lifelong slavery. The text opens almost a decade after the end of the Civil War, yet there is clear evidence that freedom is not the same as equality. Sethe has come to Ohio as a freedom seeker, or escaped slave, although she soon falls foul of the Fugitive Slave Act, which entitles the current owners of Sweet Home to pursue her from Kentucky across the Ohio River to Cincinnati. She leaves prison as a free woman only because she is deemed damaged goods.

124 Bluestone Road

The house at 124 Bluestone Road is repeatedly personified throughout the narrative. It embodies the historic griefs held in the house. Each section of the novel opens with a description of 124, which starts as 'spiteful', before becoming 'loud' as Beloved makes increasing demands. The house turns 'quiet' before the community assemble to expel the spirit of Beloved. The house is both animated and possessed by women. The house is steeped in grief; on his brief return the white owner Bodwin recalls how 'women died there; his mother, grandmother, and aunt and an older sister before he was born' (259).

Denver tells Paul D that the baby's ghost is 'lonely and rebuked'. The ghost is rejected just as the house is ignored by the community.

Despite being in the free north, 124 is haunted by slavery. The haunting is female and overshadows the benign, peripheral presence of the male owner, Edward Bodwin. He reveals many of his female relatives died in the house. As a white man he at least had privacy while Baby Suggs could not recover from the shock of 'them' in her yard. While he supports 124, Bodwin accepts black visitors at the back of his house while entertaining slave owners at the front.

Baby Suggs makes an effort to claim the house by rejecting the outside kitchen and removing the back door, which she associates with slavery. The ideal home was planned with the kitchen at the back hidden from visitors. Suggs sees this as a way of segregating hired help. This separates the working woman. Baby Suggs makes the kitchen the heart of her home. She shares with those who make 124 a way station.

Haunting is not always seen as a negative experience. The memories can be bittersweet. While Baby Suggs is deeply missed, she also provides guidance to both Sethe and Denver as they recall her lessons on life.

The house has had a more positive history as a way station providing shelter, food and information for those trying to make their way to freedom. It would have been a focal point for the community as people tried to trace relatives. There is a stark contrast between the image of 124 as a support hub and the desolate place that Paul D encounters at the start of the novel.

Denver does draw a sense of security from 124 and the surrounding land. Denver's 'emerald closet' draws on the sermons of Baby Suggs. She finds safety and reassurance in the boxwood and this is a gateway to her natural self. As in Shakespeare, the woods are sylvan and provide the freedom to think.

Sweet Home

Sweet Home features heavily in the recollections of Sethe and Paul D. These memories take place at a time considered the 'peak' of slavery. Sethe believed the Garners to be examples of benign 'slave holders'. Paul D likewise recalls how Mr Garner insisted his slaves should be treated like men, although he is more circumspect in praising the Garners.

Halle sheds Sethe's naivety about the kindness of the Garners. He reminds her that he had no choice but to buy his mother out through additional work to avoid her dying on the job. Not only did his mother Baby Suggs continue to work for the Garners while sick and lame, but by Halle vowing to stay and work to earn her freedom he was essentially condemning his own children to a life in slavery as replacement labour.

Descriptions of Sweet Home often juxtapose images of beauty and death. Sethe recalls 'although there was not a leaf on that farm that did not make her want to scream, it rolled itself out before her in shameless beauty' (18).

Sethe returns to this paradox again and again. When she remembers Sweet Home 'it made her wonder if hell was a pretty place too' (18). Within the same memory Sethe has a graphic recollection; 'boys hanging from the most beautiful sycamores in the world' (18).

While Sethe and Paul D's time at Sweet Home coincides with the closing years of sanctioned slavery, the experiences described are just as horrific and dehumanizing as in previous generations.

The Fugitive Slave Act of 1850 proves to be a tragic catalyst for the events in the novel. As an escapee from a Kentucky plantation Sethe was regarded as a fugitive. The Act allowed slave owners to work with marshals and enter into northern states where black populations were considered to be free in order to re-capture and return them to slavery. Sethe would rather end her children's lives than have them live with the degradation and cruelty of slavery.

TASK: Significance of Settings

It is worth reflecting on the following:

How does the world beyond 124's boundaries feature in the narrative?

How is the relationship between 'Sweet Home' and outside elements conceptualised and explored?

What values, qualities or possibilities are implicit or explicit here?

2.5 The *'Other'*

In this section we will;

- *Develop informed responses to Beloved, using associated concepts and terminology*
- *Analyse ways in which meanings are shaped in texts*
- *Explore literary texts informed by different interpretations*

The *'Other'*

Monster OED

A large, ugly and frightening imaginary creature. When applied to humans, "an inhumanity cruel or wicked person".

The monster is the Gothic presentation of 'the *Other'*. Society can crea monsters through 'othering'. At its root, monstrosity is based on differen and a failure to conform. Traditional myths created monsters based on wh humanity was not. Monsters were identified by animalistic features. By tl nineteenth century the monster was a product of society, in opposition rational behaviour and thought. A prime example is seen in *The Strange Ca of Dr Jekyll and Mr Hyde*, with Hyde being the manifestation of Jekyll's de and dark desires. Imperial Gothic monsters were liminal 'others', inhum yet familiar. Beloved shares some of these traits.

The Victorian or Imperial Gothic saw a humanization of the supernatural, the monster was given traits and motivations. These monsters served embodiments of fears of modernized world, often linked to developmen in science and colonialism. The Gothic monster saw elements of the ratior civilised world combine with irrational, chaotic human fantasy.

Liminality

Characteristics relating to being in transition, or occupying a position on, or at both sides of, a boundary or significant threshold. occupies a space between the human and supernatural.

The monster is also a product of humanity as they are 'birthed ' by humar developed in the author's imagination. For example, when Bram Stoker w writing *Dracula,* England was seen as the 'civilised centre'. The decline political and economic power created anxiety. The 1890s threatened ghostly return to the past. Dracula was published as the Empire was decline. There was a real fear of regressing into a primitive state. Dracula a monstrous trespasser. He materialises difference. As an immigrant I fosters a fear of the unknown. The text could be seen as the presentation atonement. Dracula enacts reverse colonialism and so may be regarded a deserved punishment for the violence enacted on other nations.

It is perhaps fitting that this critique of colonialism and Empire may provi a model for Beloved. As a daughter of slavery, she has returned to remi communities 'not to pass on' the events of the past, but to learn from the and work together to build a stronger future.

Throughout the narrative characters are seen maintaining and transgressi boundaries. Denver and Sethe are bounded by 124, while Beloved cross the boundary between the living and the dead. However, while Beloved required to prompt memory, she functions as a vampire draining Sethe vitality. Vampirism is a monstrous illness and will provide retribution f those who forget.

In appearing as a weak young woman, Beloved makes the monstrous familiar. She is presumed to be a victim of abuse and slavery. However, her clothes mark her as an outsider, suggesting she is of a higher social status. She is unable to interact in conventional ways, as she displays a child's needs and impulses, constantly craving attention.

She is something to be feared but also demands attention. She is a product of Gothic heritage. Her visions of conditions on the slave ships and the horrors suffered by earlier generations of women require a remembrance. She is transgressive in that she does not answer to conventional ethics. She seduces Paul D not out of lust but driven by jealousy of the attention he received from Sethe, and threatens Denver and Sethe when her wishes are not met. She seems irrational and therefore threatens stability. Though appearing vulnerable, she exploits Sethe's vulnerability and guilt.

While monstrous, she serves as communal scapegoat, simultaneously allowing others to remember and then forget the horrors they have lived through.

TASK: Fear in *Beloved*

Consider the ways in which Morrison creates **a sense of fear** in *Beloved*.

You must relate your discussion to relevant contextual factors and you should explore how fears are presented.

You could include:

The atmosphere in 124 in the opening chapters
Denver's fear of her mother
Paul D's fear of Beloved
Denver's experience in the cold house
Sethe's experience in the Clearing
Stamp Paid's fears as he circles 124

Part Three:
Textual Commentary and Analysis

3.1   Part I: Chapters 1-8

3.2   Part I: Chapters 9-18

3.3   Part II: Chapters 19-25

3.4   Part III: Chapters 26-28

3.1 Part I: Chapters 1-8 '124 was spiteful'

In this section we will;

- *Consider how language and imagery convey writer's intentions in Beloved*
- *Evaluate the methods employed by Morrison to convey the patterns of natural speech and thought processes*
- *To show understanding of how Morrison's choice of form, structure and language shapes meanings.*

Introduction

When responding to *Beloved,* you should consider how the writer's linguistic and literary techniques enhance or develop themes and characterisation, and how they contribute to the overall narrative style.

The novel is divided into 28 chapters. These are not numbered but for the ease of reference page references and chapter numbers have been referenced in the detailed summaries. The text is presented in three clear sections, to chart the progression of the haunting of 124.

The narrative is not linear although it is broadly chronological. There is use of interlacing narrative to provide information from various perspectives.

TASK: Structural Choices

What are the effects of drawing on a range of sources and perspectives?

What is the effect of breaks in chronology, or the representation of the same event from a different character's viewpoint?

Dedication

Morrison dedicates the novel to the *'Sixty million and more'.*

The number provides a scale which seems unimaginable. The large number suggests the immeasurable *'and more'*. The emphasis is on the painful legacy and the indirect pain generations later.

Epigraph

The epigraph is taken from the New Testament, St. Paul's letters to the Romans, verse 9. In this verse Paul has been provoking Christ's message across the Mediterranean. His letters are sent to remind new followers that

God's love comes from grace. He will give glory to those you are not 'beloved'. It is about God's grace, love and forgiveness. It also demands that one must accept grace. It highlights that God's love is for all. This epigraph does raise questions. Is Sethe playing God in naming her child 'Beloved' and in the actions that she takes.

Chapter 1 Pages 3-23   *'124 was spiteful'*

The novel opens with the enigmatic *'124 was spiteful'* (3). The house is personified as the reader is surprised by the oxymoron of the *'baby's venom'* (3). A baby is normally a site of innocence. Here the house attacks the residents due to the anger of an unnamed baby. 124 may have significance. It is the third child that is missing. Equally 124 could be an ironic reflection of the absent family; a mother, a couple, four children.

The text begins with absence and loss. The family has disintegrated – the grandmother is dead and the two sons have left home. The colloquial tone and rhythm of the language suggests an oral narrative, a story being told to expectant listeners.

Movements through time are fluid as the reader is taken back to the point where grandmother Baby Suggs is *'suspended between the nastiness of life and the meanness of the dead'* (4). It is a house oppressed by sadness and anger as a baby haunts the occupants.

Sethe remembers having to prostitute herself to the stonemason in return for the inscription 'Beloved' on her baby's headstone, recalling *'knees wide open as any grave'* (5). She seems detached from her body, not only linking it with death but with animals in the repetition of the verb *'rutting'*. There is equal detachment in the bald revelation that the baby's throat was cut. The reader then begins to question why they are rejected by a *'town full of disgust'* (5).

Sethe's memories then drift back to her time as a slave on Sweet Home. She has an ambivalent relationship to Sweet Home, recalling its *'shameless beauty'* (7) yet experiencing trauma as she recalls every leaf made her *'want to scream'* (7). Plants link to pain and trauma, suggesting it is natural.

Fellow slave Paul D appears on her doorstep after eighteen years. He is sad to hear that Baby Suggs has died and Sethe's pessimistic view that *'Being alive was the hard part'* (8). A relationship is foreshadowed in the flirtation between Sethe and Paul D on the word 'bad'.

The reader is given fragments of information which they must piece together as they progress through the text. An early example is Sethe having no information about her missing husband Halle. Paul D claims limited knowledge which he privately qualifies - *'except for the churn'* (9), information he does not share with Sethe at this stage.

Lives seem cheapened by the institution of slavery, as when Paul D recalls how the owner of Sweet Home Mrs Garner sold his brother. This seems to have shaped the characters. Paul D makes repeated references to Sethe's *'iron eyes'* (10) and remembers even in her youth she was the *'iron-eyed girl'* (12).

Sethe's adult daughter Denver resents Paul D's intrusion into 124. She notices how her mother does not look away from him and feels excluded from their reminiscences of Sweet Home. She is lonely and isolated, secretly wishing for the ghost to appear.

Paul D has experienced the presence in 124 with the negative energy on entering the house. The red light could be anger but red also suggests hearts and passion. Furniture moves in protest and he seems to defeat the ghost in his first confrontation. He is puzzled by Sethe's refusal to leave and her puzzling reason that *'It cost too much'* (18) to go. He seems to be the remedy for the haunting and is seen as 'something blessed' in his ability to make others talk about their heartaches.

The opening chapter ends with an emphasis on Denver's isolation. She misses the ghost, *'the only other company she ever had'* (23).

Chapter 2 Pages 24-33   *"How loose the silk. How fine and loose and free'*

Sethe has slept with Paul D. The initial desire has been replaced with disappointment. The reader views the scene through Paul D's perspective. He reflects on how everything has happened so quickly and they now lie *'resentful of one another...His dreaming of her had been too long and too long ago'* (25).

Sethe recalls her time with Halle. She has wanted a marriage ceremony and notes that he did not 'lay claim' to her. This is not just a comment on the fact she felt their love seemed fraternal rather than passionate, rather that he was never legally able to claim her, as marriage required a contract and Halle was already contracted as a slave to Garner.

The extensive scars on Sethe's back that he treasured moments before is now a *'revolting clump of scars'* (25). In failing to see the 'tree' in her scars he then remembers the tree he named Brother on the Sweet Home farm, which provided a comfort to him. This then prompts a memory of fellow slave Sixo, *'Indigo with a flame-red tongue'* (25), with whom he feels he cannot compare.

Sethe is equal in her immediate regret. She resents how Paul D *'tore up th house'* (26). Sethe also lets her thoughts drift back to Sweet Home and he efforts to make it more homely. She remembers Baby Suggs warning not t love. Beyond advice on the limitations of love this also indicated the cruelt of slavery, as Baby Suggs refers to those men *'who hadn't run off, or bee hanged, got rented out, loaned out, bought up, brought back, stored up mortgaged, won, stolen or seized'* (28). As Sethe and Paul D regard eacl other's backs there is a sense of looking at what is behind them. They wi build a relationship from memories.

Sethe seems to have had an exceptional experience in her *'amazing lucl* (28) of a love marriage with Baby Suggs's son Halle and all of their childrei are their own rather than products of exploitative masters. Something in he life has made Sethe bitter as she now regards herself a *'fool'* (28).

The text digresses further as the reader returns to Paul D's menta comparisons of his own union to the trials Sixo had in trying to meet up witl the Thirty Mile Woman. The text returns to Sethe's awareness of Paul [watching her, and her reflection that even when free from slavery, womei must tolerate men looking at them as though *'examining an ear of corn fo quality'* (30).

Sethe had considered Mrs Garner as kind but there is evidence that as a white woman, she is part of the institution of slavery. She is dismissive c Sethe's desire for a wedding ceremony. Sethe and Halle do mark their unioi in the cornfield. Sethe has a rare memory of happiness and liberation. In a sensory description, she conflates the memory of Halle with the beauty o the corn husks; *'How loose the silk. How fine and loose and free'* (33).

Chapter 3 Pages 34-51   *'...things she halfway told'*

Focalizer: A character through which the story is told; the story is given from their perspective.

This section is focalized through Denver – *'Denver's secrets were sweet* (34). She has a safe space, the boxwood, which keeps her *'closed off from the hurt of the hurt world'* (35). The boxwood protects her like a charm just as Sethe tries to protect her from the outside world. As in the openin chapter, Denver shares the belief that 124 is possessed and treats the house as *'a person that wept, sighed, trembled and fell into fits'* (35). We are in the supernatural world as Denver has a vision of a white dres kneeling and holding on to her mother.

Denver has been raised on the story of her birth. She recalls herself as the *'little antelope'* (36) that kicked in her mother's womb. The novel thei slides into Sethe's memories of the escape from Sweet Home. She has an image of the tree, a place of solace and peace but now the home of a lynching victim.

This is an oral narrative *'Sethe told Denver'* (36). There is a level of uncertainty regarding Sethe's own mother as she recalls *'they danced the antelope'*, linking the three generations of women. The narrative is circular. Sethe often provides an outline, withholding information for later retellings.

Sethe builds the tension as she describes hiding in fear of a boy with *'an appetite'* (38). She recalls her animal instinct to protect her unborn child, as *'something came up out of the earth into her'* (38). She remembers being *'like a snake'* (38). The fear is dispelled as an unlikely helper appears, *'the most raggedy looking* trash' (38), Amy Denver, who becomes a saviour and helps with childbirth. Her words as she massages Sethe's torn feet – *'Anything dead coming back to life hurts'* (42) - could easily describe the disturbance in 124 and also presages Beloved and how she affects Sethe and Denver. It can also be noted that while characters cannot always talk about their feelings, they can minister to each other and there is comfort provided through human touch.

The novel jolts back to the present. Denver and Sethe try to puzzle out the significance of the dress. Sethe considers how 're-memory' is a physical response, a memory that can be jolted by someone else. She urges Denver to leave the past alone. Denver is excluded from Sethe's secret, *'things she halfway told'* (45). Paul D's presence encourages Sethe to plan. There are memories of Baby Suggs and the lack of colour in her own life. Sethe recognises that she misses and yearns for her boys. After sharing memories Sethe retreats to silence while Paul D sings. Now she considers the way Paul D *'broke up the place'* could provide room for life.

Paul D 's songs recall the Georgia chain gang where he suffered further indignity. His memories are touched upon before Sethe permits him to *'scramble'* (50). She is still uncomfortable with his desire to explore past memories; *'To Sethe, the future was a matter of keeping the past at bay'* (51). She does not reveal her secret to Paul D but hints in references to 'schoolteacher' finding her and Denver joining her with the rats, a thinly veiled reference to jail.

Chapter 4 Pages 52-59   *'A life. Could be'*

Paul D challenges Sethe for constantly defending Denver's rudeness, suggesting Denver should take responsibility for her own words and actions as she is grown. Paul D suggests that it is risky and dangerous for any ex-slave woman to love her children too much;

'The best thing, he knew, was to love just a little bit...' (54).

Sethe is further angered when Paul D asks Denver if her mother has been with other men. She wavers in her feelings and wants to go back to how it was before his arrival. She doesn't want to risk reflecting on feelings inside her. There is use of extended dialogue as the conflict escalates, but there is a shift towards hope and unity as Paul D offers to hold her and make '*a life*' (55).

He proposes a visit to the carnival, itself a site for illusion. Denver sulks at first but eventually comes around. This is a positive step for Sethe yet the walk there is filled with images of danger and decay. This perhaps serves to foreshadow revelations of killing later. There are also references to hanging which prevent the day out being sentimental.

Despite the stench of the dying roses, there is hope that Sethe and Denver can re-join the community. Sethe is encouraged by the linked shadows as a sign of the future, '*A life. Could be*' (57) as '*the shadows of three people still held hands*' (59).

Chapter 5 Pages 60-67   '*A fully dressed woman walked out of the water.*'

This section begins with the unusual image of a woman emerging from the water. She reaches 124 before collapsing under a tree. Sethe's immediate urge to pass water is linked to '*water breaking from a breaking womb*' (61), subconsciously linking back to childbirth. The young woman is like an infant, with hands and feet that are '*soft and new*' (62). They assume she has escaped from some form of enslavement or abuse and take her inside to recover. She introduces herself as Beloved in a '*low and rough*' (62) voice. Sethe makes a connection to the headstone and this prompts her to help. Here Boy has disappeared, a small detail which suggests the supernatural, as dogs are supposed to react to haunting.

Denver also feels a desire to tend Beloved '*out of love and a breakneck possession*' (64). Beloved craves sugar; 'It was as though sweet things were what she was born for' (66). While her appetite is healthy, she moves like an old woman. Paul D is suspicious about her. He cannot understand how she can act sick but have '*good skin, bright eyes and* (be) *strong as a bull*' (67).

Chapter 6 Pages 68-75 '*Sethe was licked, tasted, eaten by Beloved's eyes*'

Beloved has come between Beloved and Sethe. Beloved devours Sethe's company; '*Sethe was licked, tasted, eaten by Beloved's eyes*' (68). The text suggests that Beloved may be a product of witchcraft; her behaviour hints she is '*Like a familiar*' (68). There is a supernatural element to the shadows that form on the walls as they '*clashed and crossed on the ceiling like black* swords' (69). There is something unnatural about her interactions as Sethe describes her touch as '*loaded...with desire*' (69). Beloved would seem to embody the '*unheimleich*', or uncanny. She encourages storytelling and orality. She begs Sethe in her own imperfect speech '*Tell me your diamonds*' (69). There is a link between a love of sweets and storytelling as it is noted that voicing memories '*became a way to feed her*' (69). While Sethe's memories cause pain Beloved seems nourished by them.

Sethe finds the memories can hurt yet being able to share these with Beloved creates an '*unexpected pleasure*' (70). She remembers her desire for a wedding and the earrings that she was given – '*They said it was all right*' (70). Beloved asks her about her mother and it is realised that she was marked by exile and loss. Sethe finds she has forgotten her mother's language. Sethe is overwhelmed as she rushes to fold sheets, recalling Nan and her mother on the pile of bodies. Denver is jealous of Sethe's past and curious about how Beloved knows these things. She is uncomfortable with Beloved's seeming obsession with Sethe.

Chapter 7 Pages 76-86 '*Beloved was shining...*'

Paul D has concerns about Beloved- '*Beloved was shining and Paul D didn't like it*' (76). Sethe and Denver bristle at his interference, '*sending out sticky spiderwebs to touch one another*' (77). Paul D compares Beloved to a slippery fish. He then digresses to his own movements over the years. He returns to the present, noting that Beloved made an appearance right at the moment they had been acting like a family. He has empathy for women faced by the real terror of the Klan – '*the dragon swam the Ohio at will*' (79).

124 has served as a way station and a safe haven for wandering spirits and weary travellers. When Baby Suggs was alive, it provided clothing, food and a place to leave messages.

Sethe and Paul D are on the verge on another fight. It is evidence of Beloved's indirect influence that an argument about her prompts Sethe's memories of Halle. The short sharp dialogue reflects the tension in the room. Sethe scoffs that Paul D would be the first man who didn't mistreat a woman. She even blames Halle on abandoning his children. Paul D then reveals that Halle must have seen Sethe as the boys were stealing milk from her and it 'broke him'. He has pieced this together when Sethe told the story of the assault. Paul D defends Halle's memory when he protests '*A man ain't a goddamn ax*' (81).

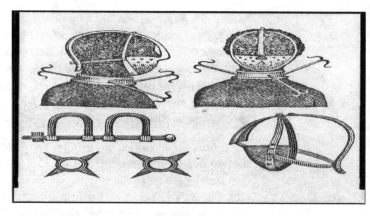

Paul D couldn't tell Sethe at Sweet Home as he had '*a bit in my mouth*' (82). This reference reveals the brutal treatment of slaves. Sethe is angry that he has given her even more images of pain to store with her own memories; '*her brain was not interested in the future*' (83). She does recognise his pain and responds with a maternal touch. Knees are kneaded like bread in the restaurant, Sethe regarding it as the 'serious work of beating back the past'.

Sethe does not discuss with Paul D directly but wonders if the bit contributes to the wildness she sometimes sees in his eyes. She recognises his songs and metaphors are a vital tool at times when he is not ready to discuss experiences. Paul D has also been repressing his memories. She offers to listen, as he confesses the anger felt on watching Mister the rooster;

'*I was something else and that something was less than a chicken sitting in the sun on a tub*' (86).

The chapter closes with this vivid image, which powerfully captures the moment when Paul D, though a man, realises he is seen as property and less than human by another person.

Chapter 8 Pages 87-100   *Upstairs Beloved was dancing'*

As Sethe and Paul D work through difficult memories '*Upstairs Beloved was dancing*' (87). While a picture of joy, the imagery is wintry as Denver feels '*cold and light as a snowflake*' (87). The girls are '*merry as kittens*' (88). Denver seeks to catch a glimpse of the scar on Beloved's throat. This informs the reader that Beloved may be the long-dead baby returned. Denver believes Beloved is something other than human. She risks the question '*What's it like over there?*'.

Beloved's response makes reference to hot and cramped conditions, and dead bodies. This signifies a hellish purgatory, which is disrupted by reference to a bridge. This reference is not immediately clear but is later elucidated when Beloved describes the horrific conditions for women on slave ships on the Middle Passage.

Beloved does not deny Denver's theories. She gives a reason for return which is *'to see her face'* (88). The voice becomes that of a distressed child as she complains *'She left me behind. By myself'* (89). She promises to stay at 124; *'This is where I am'* (89). Her possessive nature is for Sethe alone – *'You can go but she is the one I have to have'* (89). Beloved turns on Denver and repeats *'Don't...never tell me what to do'* (89). She quickly makes peace with Denver asking her to tell the story of her birth.

Denver's 'sister-girl' keeps her from the box wood. She gives her *'a racing heart, dreaminess, society, danger, beauty'* (90). Denver crafts her story with care. She understands the importance of it. She aims *'to construct out of the strings she had heard all her life a net to hold Beloved'* (90). The reader can appreciate how Denver's re-telling is woven from her mother's version.

TASK: Exploring the text

Compare Denver's account of her birth with the earlier account provided by Sethe.

Denver feeds Beloved with her story, while Beloved helps Denver *'see what she was saying'* (91). This creates empathy for what her mother went through at nineteen. Denver elaborates; this then blends into a presentation of the event through dialogue and a return to Sethe's perspective. In Sethe's version Amy Denver reveals how she was given to Mr Buddy, showing vulnerable poor white women were also treated like property. In Sethe's extended memory, Amy sings Sethe a lullaby. The historical nature of this song indicates that Amy's heritage may have been of a higher social status than her current poverty. In a novel where many names have symbolic functions it can be noted that Amy derives from *'amor'* and she shows love through healing and supportive touch.

Pathetic fallacy links Sethe and her family with nature. She is guided on her escape by thoughts of her children or her 'four summer stars'. Sethe can envy the seeds in the ground that 'sleep confident of a future'.

Sethe's water breaking in the river acts as a baptism. The chapter ends with *'two throwaway people'* (100) and the explanation that Amy provided Denver with her name.

Illustration from *Uncle Tom's Cabin*: 'Eliza Crossed the Ohio...'

3.1 Chapters 9-18 *'It was time to lay it all down'*

In this section we will;

- *Consider how language and imagery convey writer's intentions in Beloved*
- *Evaluate the methods employed by Morrison to convey the patterns of natural speech and thought processes*
- *To show understanding of how Morrison's choice of form, structure and language shapes meanings.*

Chapter 9 Pages 101-124   *'It was time to lay it all down'*

Sethe misses the comfort and guidance of Baby Suggs. They have learnt the force of silence. They choose to stay quiet about their pain. Once in her life Sethe told, when she revealed maltreatment to Mrs Garner, and for that she was brutally whipped by schoolteacher, leaving her with the tree of her back.

Sethe recalls Baby Suggs's whispering how *'It was time to lay it all down'* (101). Resignation becomes one of *'her heavy knives of defence against misery'* (101). Baby Suggs remembers 124 before it became a plaything of the spirits. There was evidence of cheer. The house was a place of rest and Baby Suggs a source of information. Baby Suggs becomes a preacher. She teaches herself and provides a new type of faith as she *'took her great heart to the Clearing'* (102). The community runs to her, as she encourages them to laugh, dance and cry. In a blending of religious conventions, she becomes a mythic priestess. She did not preach of sin or blessings. Instead she encourages the community to envision grace as only *'the grace they could imagine'* (103).

Baby Suggs places an emphasis on all reclaiming their own bodies. To do so is to reclaim humanity. She proclaims all *'flesh that weeps, laughs'* (103). Her message is simple *'...love it. Love it hard. Yonder they do not love your flesh. They despise it...* (103). She recognises the damage inflicted by the white slave owners, who are 'other'. Baby Suggs encourages men, women and children to dance and sing. They must celebrate and reclaim their own bodies.

Sethe recalls these meetings in the Clearing but then feels anger and frustration that in resigning herself to deterioration and death she had *'proved herself a liar'* and *'dismissed her great heart'* (104). Baby Suggs reveals her despair and horror that *'Those white things have taken all I had or dreamed'* (104).

It is after the death of Baby Suggs that the house feels the full force of *'the venom of its ghost'* (105). Sethe hints that Baby Suggs's heart gave up 28 days after Sethe's arrival at 124.

Sethe's recollections of Baby Suggs prompt her to take Beloved and Denver to the Clearing. While there she is overcome with the memory of being helped across the Ohio river. She was helped by Stamp Paid, Ella and John. In seeing the newborn baby, Ella warns Sethe *'Don't love nothing'* (108).

There is a detailed description of Baby Suggs tending Sethe on her arrival at 124. There is horror as she notices the *'roses of blood'* coming through the blanket placed on Sethe's back. This is juxtaposed with the moment of happiness she experiences as she is reunited with her children. Sethe recalls that the month following her arrival at 124 *'Bit by bit...she had claimed herself'* (111). She notes that freedom from slavery does not bring peace; *'Freeing yourself was one thing; claiming ownership of that freed self was another'* (111-112).

The return to the Clearing foreshadows death with images of baby's spit and oily blood mingling. Sethe has accepted that Halle has gone but wishes for the comfort of the hands of Baby Suggs and her *'long-distance love'* (112). Sethe recognises the information Paul D provides may replace her previous anger and resentment, but struggles with her *'new pictures and old rememories that broke her heart'* (112) and gave her a *'brand new sorrow'* (112).

Sethe is aware that in the past others may have shared her grief but after the arrival of the baby ghost *'she returned their disapproval with the potent pride of the mistreated'* (112). Paul D may know be there to share things with her but brought *'another kind of haunting'* (113).

There is an abrupt return to the present as Sethe feels as though she is being strangled. Denver rushed to save her. It is a moment which is uncanny as there is evidence of bruises on her neck. Beloved's touch initially gives relief and Sethe has a *'glimpse of happiness'* (114) and can picture a future with Paul D which would give her the strength to deal with her memories. There is a sense other people have been destroyed by their memories.

Sethe questions how she seemed to have managed alone but now seems to be struggling when there are others ready to share with her. There is a moment of peace and *'Beloved fingers were heavenly'* (114). She is troubled when Beloved begins to kiss her neck and scolds that she is too old for that type of interaction. Initially it suggests a taboo relating to inappropriate contact but Sethe's memory is more unsettling as she recalls that she recoiled *'because the girl's breath was exactly like new milk'* (115). At this point she remembers Baby Suggs's hands and knows that this was not the sensation she had as she was choking. What she has felt has been identical to '*touches from the other side*' (116). Despite this new knowledge Sethe dismisses the links between Beloved and the baby's ghost. As she leaves the Clearing, she knows she wants to build a life with Paul D; '*the story was bearable because it was his as well*' (116).

As the focus shifts back to Denver, she is seen as both dulled and sharpened by her solitude. There is a sympathy between Denver and Beloved. Meanwhile, Sethe aspires '*to launch her newer, stronger life with a tender man*' (117).

Beloved is unhappy that Sethe's attention is with '*Him mostly*' (118). Denver follows her to the stream and accuses her of choking Sethe. Denver suffers from misplaced memories, '*Once upon a time she had known more and wanted to*' (119). She recalls standing outside Lady Jones's house. She attended lessons there for almost a year. She had not noticed the others avoiding her. This hints at something monstrous. The '*crawling?already girl*' is now identified as her dead sister.

Denver chooses to hide from Paul D and Sethe in the '*emerald closet*' (123). The reader is not told Nelson's question until close to the end of the chapter. Denver confirms for the reader that she believes in '*the miraculous resurrection of Beloved*' (123).

Chapter 10 Pages 125-133 '*love songs to Mr Death*'

The chapter opens with third person limited perspective as Paul D recalls moving away from the rooster. He is sent to the chain gang for trying to kill Brandywine, his owner after Sweet Home. There is a sense of parallel between Sethe and Paul D, who both make epic journeys. Paul D in particular recalls Odysseus in his long and circuitous wanderings before arriving at 124.

As Paul D is sent to Georgia for the attempted murder of Brandywine, the prospect of the chain gang makes Paul D '*tremble*' (125). The imagery recalls the grave, as the men are kept chained in wooden boxes set into the ground. He cannot make his hands stop shaking to eat. The guards terrorise the men; no one spoke, '*at least not with words*' (126). As with Sethe's humiliation there is a link made between feeding and assault as the guards make the men ask for '*breakfast*' (127). Paul D recalls the intuition of the 'Hiii!' man, who was able to disrupt this when he felt prisoners could bear no more.

Paul D sardonically personifies '*the flirt whom folks called life for leading them on*' (128) and recalls their '*love songs to Mr Death*' (128).

The men work collectively, communicating feelings through work songs and 'chain-danced' their way to survival when heavy rain and floods threaten to create a landslide; '*the chain that held them would save all or none'(130)* and '*they talked through that chain like Sam Morse'*(130). Paul D emerges from the mudslide as though escaping from the underworld. The extraordinary escape is presented in the style of a fairy tale, with movements charted with a repeated reference to travelling 'past the…' various natural features.

The men find saviours in the Cherokee, a people who have also been damaged by settlers and decimated by illnesses caught from those who stole their land. The Cherokee help the men get on their way again. Paul D remains, out of indecision and a lack of a place to call home. When he leaves, he follows the advice to follow the flowers. He recalls his relationship with the weaver lady, how '*he crawled into her bed crying*' (133). He has little more to say about this eighteen-month long relationship. He stores his memories '*into the tobacco tin lodged in his chest*' (133).

Chapter 11 Pages 136-138 *'She moved him'*

Chapters 9-11 have shown how characters have dealt with pain. The chapter opens '*She moved him*' (134). This seems ambiguous as Paul D realises '*he was moving out of 124*' (134). This is blamed on the 'house fits' (135) rather than Sethe '*whom he loved a little bit more every day*' (136). He begins to sleep on the chair, then the keeping room, before making his way outside to the store room and the cold house. It is becoming clear that the 'she 'in the opening of the chapter is not Sethe. There is a moment of tension as the reader realises it is Beloved; '*She came, and he wanted to knock her* down' (136). There is a hint at her supernatural nature, as he puzzles that '*He should have been able to hear her breathing*' (137). She demands a physical union, '*On the inside part. And you have to call me my name*' (137). The reference to looking back recalls Lot's wife, turned to pillar of salt for daring to look at evil.

He is appalled with the way his body responds to her but realises that the act chips away at his '*tobacco tin*' (138) heart. At this point, Beloved's sexuality complicates the reading of her returned self as a ghost or spirit. It is possible here she represents the need to engage with history, just as later she will serve as a collective memory.

Chapter 12 Pages 139-146 *'This is the place I am'*

The novel shifts to Denver's perspective as she contemplates her need for Beloved's attention; '*To go back to the original hunger was impossible*' (139). When Beloved does make eye contact, she considers her feelings of isolation and anger when feeling as though she is *'Not seen'* (139). Denver's language conveys a need and desire for an emotional connection.

Denver asks Beloved questions and is not wholly satisfied with the vague answers that she receives. Beloved has restricted memories of a white man, losing her mother and a bridge. This would seem to fit with Sethe's theory that Beloved had been locked in the home of a white man. This in turn prompts an omniscient digression regarding Ella's imprisonment.

Denver has guessed why Beloved has gone to the cold house but she still feeds Beloved stories to keep her occupied, and chooses to keep this information from Sethe. She is frustrated that *'Beloved has eyes only for Sethe'* (143). She senses Beloved's sugary breath as the girls move around the cold house. Although it is noon, the cold house remains in darkness. There is a moment of panic when Beloved disappears. This would seem to confirm that Beloved is a ghost. Denver feels at her most isolated;

'Now she is crying because she has no self' (145).

Beloved reappears and affirms *'This is the place I am'* (146). The 'minnows of light' are transformed to 'sunlit cracks' when Beloved is seen. Beloved tries to explain herself as a darkness or absence. Just as the baby had no name, here Beloved becomes all the faceless and nameless 'disappeared' lost through slavery. She disturbs Denver as she curls up and moans on the floor. This coupled with water imagery suggests that Denver is given a vicarious experience of the conditions on the slave ships. Denver feels as though she is drowning. Beloved in this chapter becomes the overwhelming power of the past, even for those like Denver with no direct experience of slavery.

Chapter 13 Pages 147-156 *'They were only Sweet Home men at Sweet Home'*

Paul D accepts he is the *'last of the Sweet Home men'* (147). He considers how they were treated as men. He notes that there was no point reading *'since nothing important to them could be put down on paper'* (147).

He questions his own manhood as he is named by a white man. Garner may have given them merit but schoolteacher taught truth, *'they were only Sweet Home men at Sweet Home'* (147). He equally questions his masculinity in his inability to refuse Beloved's advances. He has had many challenges in life but has felt the most shame in his behaviour with Beloved.

He makes plans to tell Sethe. He expresses worries that Beloved is not a girl *'but something in disguise'* (149). When he meets Sethe he expresses a desire to make her pregnant. This is a spontaneous idea driven by a need to direct her towards the future. He also recognises this would be *'a way to*

hold on to her, document his manhood and break out of the girl's spell' (151).
He directs his anger towards Beloved and won't let '*no motherless gal*' (152)
ruin his future. He goes further in his anger, terming her a '*lazy, stray pup of
a woman*' (152).

Beloved interrupts their moments of happiness and tries to hug Sethe. This
leaves him 'icy cold'. Paul is equally wary of Denver's interventions, asking
her '*And whose ally you?*' (153). While Sethe does invite him back to bed, he
is concerned about the intensity of her relationship with her children
'*Unless carefree, mother love was a killer*' (155). Sethe, in her turn, feels he
resents her children. It is also at this time that Sethe realises Beloved may be
a revenant and her baby returned in adult form.

The chapter has been undercut by images of dismemberment, evoked when
Sethe throws out the scraps from the restaurant. There are also patterns of
union and disunion. The snow will restrict movement as disaster looms.

Chapter 14 Pages 157-158 '*She would fly apart*'

The third person limited narrative places the reader with Beloved as she
pulls out a tooth. Beloved relies on Sethe for a physical presence.

She fears '*One of these mornings…she would fly apart*' or '*find herself in
pieces*' (157). She seems fearful that she has lost control when Paul D returns
to Sethe's bed.

Chapter 15 Pages 159-173:

The reader is taken back in time through the perspective of the minor
character Stamp Paid. It is shortly after Sethe's arrival at 124 and he has
decided to gather berries for the family.

Baby Suggs decides to make pies with the berries to show her gratitude. This
grows to a party for 90 people. Despite bringing food themselves, the guests
wake up angry the following day. Baby Suggs had '*Too much, they thought*'
(161). She had been given formal emancipation, or manumission, from
slavery, in return for her son Halle buying her freedom through additional
work. She has a two-story house and has members of her family with her.
This seems to be too much good fortune for one person and the lack of
warning given is prompted by jealousy.

The perspective shifts to Baby Suggs who has a premonition, or an odd sense
of '*the scent of their disapproval*' (162). She finds herself thinking of her lost
children. She returns to memories of her own time at Sweet Home. Here
Morrison notes that benevolent masters may do more harm than good by

shielding slaves from the harsh reality of the wider institution of slavery. Baby Suggs appreciates how it can be degrading to treat adults as children. Garner has devalued the relation Baby Suggs has with her husband in advising her to keep her slave name Jenny Whitlow rather than her chosen name.

The chapter ends with foreshadowing as Baby Suggs repeats her fear of a *'dark and coming thing'* (173).

Chapter 16 Pages 174-181

The image of thorns in the previous chapter presage the suffering in this chapter. They may represent the barbed jealousy of the neighbours who see trouble coming but do not warn the women of 124.

There is an allusion to the biblical apocalypse *'when the four horsemen came'* (174); the legacy of that day may well have elements of Famine, War, Pestilence and Death. The chapter opens from the perspective of the slavecatchers. They are the modern horsemen, with the schoolteacher being dangerous rationality, the slave catcher profit, the nephew the abuser and the sheriff representative of an unjust law.

100 DOLLARS
REWARD!

Ranaway from the subscriber on the 27th of July, my Black Woman, named

EMILY,

Seventeen years of age, well grown, black color, has a whining voice. She took with her one dark calico and one blue and white dress, a red corded gingham bonnet; a white striped shawl and slippers. I will pay the above reward if taken near the Ohio river on the Kentucky side, or THREE HUNDRED DOLLARS, if taken in the State of Ohio, and delivered to me near Lewisburg, Mason County, Ky.   THO'S. H. WILLIAMS.
August 4, 1853.

There is a labelling of slaves as 'them' and those caught are compared to children. Derogatory labels are used a slave is considered to be worth less than an animal, as they *'could not be skinned for profit and was not worth his own dead weight in coin'* (175). Schoolteacher laments that Sethe has now *'gone wild'* (176). He compares her to horses and dogs. He chides his nephews that they have beaten her *'beyond the point of education'* (176).

The chapter exposes the prejudices of the search party, as they feel what they witness is evidence of *'the cannibal life they preferred'* (177). There is no recognition that this was the act of a mother cornered.

Baby Suggs is shocked and angered by Sethe's actions. She makes Sethe nurse Denver. Sethe has shocked the locals by holding her head high when taken away by the sheriff. The community do not express the usual consolation or support of songs, just *'no words. Humming. No words at all'* (179). The reader is presented with the full horror of murder.

Chapter 17 Pages 181-186 *'That ain't her mouth'*.

The chapter opens in media res, as Paul D insists *'That ain't her mouth'*. Paul D and Stamp Paid are at the slaughterhouse. Stamp Paid shows Paul D the news clipping. Paul D can't read but knows there is *'no way in hell a black face could appear in a newspaper if the story was about something anybody wanted to hear'* (183). Stamp Paid tries to explain why the town did not warn Sethe of the approaching search party, recalling how she flew with her children *'like a lark on the wing'* (185).

Paul D is in denial. He shows Sethe the clipping in the hope that she'll laugh and dismiss it as a joke. This chapter has images of death and subversion of nature as the moment of revelation approaches.

Chapter 18 Pages 187-195 *'Your love is too thick'*

The chapter opens with Sethe trying to tell her story. She feels as though she has lost control, *'She was spinning. Round and round the room'* (187). Here Sethe is dancing and moving while Paul D is silent, an inversion of previous roles.

Paul D is dizzy with her digressions; She is *'circling him the way she was circling the subject'* (189). She tries to explain her love for her children. Her strength was to escape and to protect her children. He cannot understand this as in his view *'you protected yourself and loved small'* (191). Sethe tries to explain how her response to schoolteacher's hat was automatic, 'wings' in her head while she heard her voice say *'No.NoNo. Nononono'* (192). She calmly explains that she *'put my babies where they'd be safe'* (193). Paul D is horrified that Sethe talks about love and babies like other women yet *'what Sethe had done was what she claimed. It scared him'* (193). He can still look at her with love.

Paul D's reaction is instinctive; *'Your love is too thick'* (193). His reaction is one of horror and disbelief. He has been dehumanised before but cannot comprehend Sethe's actions. In his shock, he draws on the imagery that the white owners employ, as he reminds her that she is not an animal – *'You got two feet, Sethe, not four'* (194). The chapter highlights the moral ambiguity that surrounds actions in the novel.

TASK: Crossing Boundaries

To what extent does Morrison suggest that Beloved has journeyed to a world beyond Cincinnati society?

3.3 Part II: Chapters 19-25   *'124 WAS LOUD'*

In this section we will;

- *Consider how language and imagery convey writer's intentions in Beloved*
- *Evaluate the methods employed by Morrison to convey the patterns of natural speech and thought processes*
- *To show understanding of how Morrison's choice of form, structure and language shapes meanings.*

Chapter 19 Pages 199-235

The second part of the novel tells us *'124 WAS LOUD'* (199). Emotions are in turmoil as the house is governed by horror and disruption. Stamp Paid attempts to return to 124. While he felt it was his duty to tell Paul D the truth, he is worried about Sethe and the fact it may be seen as a betrayal.

He has always known the secrets of others. He ran messages in the war and hid runaways. He thinks about his own motives and feels bad that in punishing Sethe he was punishing Denver as well. He tries to convince himself that he is the reason Denver is alive, as in staying over and chopping wood he was in a position to save some of the children. His conscience is not clear *'And right there was the thorn'* (201).

He feels his inaction over the years has been an insult to the memory of Baby Suggs, *'the mountain to his sky'* (201). He had visited only once since the *'Misery (which is what he called Sethe's rough response to the Fugitive Bill'* (201). In the midst of this it is remembered that Baby Suggs was not even buried where she wished in the Clearing, due to *'some rule the whites had invented'* (201).

Stamp Paid reflected on the role of pride in the split between Sethe and the community. Others refused to enter 124, so Sethe refused to attend the burial service although she did stand at the grave silently. The townspeople came to the wake in the yard, but refused to eat Sethe's food. Baby Suggs had preached harmony, yet this *'was buried amid a regular dance of pride fear, condemnation and spite'* (202). Sethe's pride was regarded as hubris and she was ostracized for this.

The rest of the town wanted Sethe to fall on bad times due to *'her outrageous claims, her self-sufficiency'* (202). Stamp Paid can admit to himself he may have shared this view. He originally felt his own pain absolved him from helping. He approaches the house now. expecting anger but willing to help rid 124 of this '*stepped up haunting*' (202). He hears a '*conflagration of hasty voices*' (202), the fire imagery suggesting a subversion of the Holy Spirit. The word 'mine' is heard above the rest. Stamp Paid struggles to control his surprise that the door of 124 is shut to him. Having helped so many, he feels comfortable entering any house but is reluctant here. He does not want to knock, so leaves.

There is a parallel narrative. Stamp Paid's guilt alternates with Sethe's memories of Sweet Home. While Stamp Paid has been returning over the week but failing to knock the door, Sethe has been trying to find peace. She lists memories of discussing things with others – '*Those twenty-eight happy days were followed by eighteen years of disapproval and a solitary life*' (204). Her short time with Paul D gave her '*a few months of the sun-splashed life*' (204).

Sethe is determined to go skating despite being '*the woman junkheaped for the third time*' (205). As they skated, '*Nobody saw them falling*' (205). There are images of freedom as their '*skirts flew like wings*' (205). Sethe laughs then cries.

Beloved is still childlike- '*You finished with your eyes*' (206). Beloved hums a song. Sethe realises – '*the click came*' (206). The image of the jewel casket reinforces a fairy tale element. There is the joy of recognition; '*the magic lies in the fact that you knew it was there all along*' (208).

The narrative introduces tokens before revealing significance. The reader is told Stamp Paid is '*fingering a ribbon and smelling skin*' (208) but its relevance is not revealed at this moment.

Stamp Paid reflects on loss of faith and how Baby Suggs '*had been mocked and rebuked by the bloodspill in her backyard*' (208). Regarding Baby Suggs, he felt Sethe had caused her decline, '*He believed then that shame put her in the bed*' (208). The chapter considers themes of responsibility and blame.

However, current events make him realise she was worn out from life's struggles. He recalls meeting Baby Suggs and *rather than sadness, saw* '*indifference lodged where sadness should have been*' (209). Stamp Paid begs her to return to the Clearing and '*say the Word!*'.

Baby Suggs counters that her retreat and obsession with colour is a '*want to fix on something harmless in the world*' (211). She does not blame God, and denies the power of the 'whitefolks' yet cannot recover from the fact that '*they came in my yard*' (211). Baby Suggs is left at the back door of a house while a customer pays her a dime for mending shoes.

Stamp Paid recalls how Baby Suggs did not approve of or condemn Sethe's actions but had struggled with the idea that her world was compromised even with freedom;

'The whitefolks had tired her out at last. And him. Eighteen seventy-four and whitefolks were still on the loose' (212).

Stamp Paid here links the events at 124 with the continued violence enacted upon the black population. He lists the atrocities, which include lynchings, whippings, arson destroying schools and rapes. Even though northern states should represent freedom, 'He smelled skin, skin and hot blood' (212).

He links physical decay with moral and social rot; *'The stench stank. Stank up off the pages of the North Star'* (212).

The North Star Newspaper

An abolitionist paper published in Rochester, New York by Frederick Douglass. The paper began publishing on December 3rd 1847 and continued until merging with the Liberty Party Paper in 1851. The paper's slogan expressed the key belief in equality:

'Right is of no Sex – Truth of no Color – God is the Father of use all, and all we are Brethren'.

Stamp Paid has revealed his breaking point in encountering *'a red ribbon knotted around a curl of we woolly hair, clinging to its bit of scalp'* (213). He cannot comprehend the evil inflicted on one group of people by another. He expressed true horror; *'What are these people? You tell me, Jesus. What are they?'* (213).

The reader is transported once more to the door of 124. Stamp Paid believes the noises are the voices of those killed violently. It is a cacophony of sound; *'what a roaring'* (213).

The narrative then jumps to Sethe's newfound joy in discovering Beloved's identity. She is able to smile but is beginning to lose her connection with the wider world, choosing to be late for work for the first time ever. The women form a human trinity as Denver, Beloved and Sethe. Sethe rejects Paul D's invite to join the community declaring *'The world is in this room'* (215).

There is an ominous threat although Sethe remains oblivious; *'she neither saw the prints nor heard the voices that ringed 124 like a noose'* (214). The dead both console and oppress. The narrative seems to shift into first person as Sethe asserts *'I don't have to remember nothing'* (216).

In the meantime, Stamp Paid is trying to puzzle out the identity of the mystery girl. The narrative presents an initial digression explaining why he changed his name from Joshua. It is a bitter memory. He is forced to see his wife become the sexual property of his master's son and for that he feels he has paid his dues to the world. Stamp paid.

Stamp Paid seeks information from Ella. He is shocked to find Paul D sleeping at the church. He confronts Ella when she blames Paul D for not asking for help and creating his own difficulties. Stamp Paid is furious and holds his anger until someone *'leastways act like a Christian'* (218).

Ella reveals her misgivings about Sethe. She believed that Sethe had tricked Baby Suggs into taking her in and comments that Halle never did show up. Her animosity is also guided by fear of supernatural. She cannot believe that a white woman would help Sethe with Denver's birth. She suggests a ghost must have been involved; *'it's something I don't want no part of!'* (221).

Ella reveals she could trust Paul D a little more now that she knows he was a friend of Halle and Baby Suggs at Sweet Home. She then tells Stamp Paid about her suspicions relating to the new girl; *'people who die bad don't stay in the ground'* (221).

The reader returns to Sethe, who seems oblivious to the mounting anger of her white boss. She thinks back to the earrings donated by Mrs. Garner and the help of Amy Denver and determines to bury these memories.

Sethe has been involved in stealing from Sawyers in order to avoid the shame of queuing behind the white shoppers in the local store for her provisions. This recalls Sixo's theft of the stoat. Sixo rarely spoke but at that point argues with schoolteacher that this was not stealing but *'improving our property'* (224); if he eats the food, he will be fitter and be able to work harder. Sethe remembers that *'schoolteacher beat him anyway to show him that definitions belonged to the definers – not the defined'* (225).

Schoolteacher punished them by taking their guns so couldn't then hunt for game. Sixo argued that they had to steal to add to diet.

Sethe is aware of her motivation for stealing and *'despised herself for the pride'* (225) that made her steal. Sawyer is seen to be losing patience with her and it is suggested that he blames her entire race after death of his son in the war. Sethe seems oblivious and has an imagined dialogue with Beloved as she rushes home. She has a memory of playing with beloved as a baby in the grape arbor at Sweet Home. Sethe goes to the kitchen to fetch muslin to use as an insect net and overhears schoolteacher's 'lessons', clearly hearing her own name. It is at this point that she discovers they are listing her 'human' and 'animal' characteristics. She has a memory of feeling '*like someone was sticking fine needles into my scalp*' (228).

Sethe asks Halle about the differences between the Garners and other masters. She points out that they speak gently although Halle is quick to highlight '*what they say is the same*' (231). Schoolteacher decides that Halle has to remain on Sweet Home. Halle fears that worried that schoolteacher will seek repayment of the remaining year of debt in another way. All are aware that before schoolteacher came, Mrs. Garner had sold Paul F to raise money. Lives are commodities, even at Sweet Home. This is even more apparent when schoolteacher arrives, '*talking soft and watching hard*' (232). Sethe makes a brief allusion to Paul A being among the trees. This prompts her to send her children ahead so there would be '*no notebook for my babies*' (233). The true capacity for violence is shown when Seth confirms that Paul A had been strung up on the tree '*but not his feet or his head*' (233).

Sethe is back in the present and is cheered by the chimney of her home. Beloved is a gift, '*a body returned to her*' (233). There is an abrupt switch to Stamp Paid as he listens to '*undecipherable language*', convinced he is hearing '*the black and angry dead*' (234).

Stamp Paid makes an interesting observation about educated black individuals. They also suffer, as they have to use their intelligence and also '*had the weight of the whole race sitting there*' (234). He muses '*you needed two heads for that*' (234).

He considers the racist beliefs of many of the white population, who thought '*under every dark skin was a jungle*' (234). The imagery recalls a predatory vampire, describing the fear of '*red gums ready for their sweet white blood*' (234). Stamp Paid considered the ironic truth in the negative stereotype. A lifetime of frustration and having your humanity questioned would suggest '*the deeper and more tangled the jungle grew inside*' (234). However, any regression to violent or primal behaviour was a result of the jungle the '*whitefolks planted in them*' (234). Stamp Paid reveals that the violent animals are the white supporters of slavery;

'*The screaming baboon lived under their own white skin; the red gums were their own*' (234).

He hears the mumbling in 124. Sethe now believes she has true freedom but she is not only repressed by the voices of the dead but '*the thoughts of the women of 124, unspeakable thoughts, unspoken*' (235).

Chapter 20 Pages 236-241 'Beloved, she my daughter. She mine.

The chapter opens in first person. Sethe seems to celebrate *'Beloved, she my daughter. She mine.'* (236).

The following chapters are characterised by the highly stylized language and the dense patterns of imagery and allusion throughout.

There is a paradox in Sethe's rationale. She feels that if she had not killed Beloved, the child would have perished in slavery. Sethe thinks Beloved will understand her actions.

There is a focus on milk and maternal imagery. She was denied her own mother's milk and nursed by Nan only after the white children had been fed. Sethe is proud that she had milk for her daughter even though her memory is tinged with the assault in which her milk was taken *'like I was the cow'* (237).

Sethe can recognise her own strength in her ability to last and endure. The importance of memory is stressed in Sethe's employment of the word as a verb; she would *'lose sight of some things and memory others'* (237).

Mrs Garner does not seem to know who Sethe is. She calls her Jenny as Sethe later explains how schoolteacher has beaten her; *'Somebody had to know it. Hear it. Somebody.'* (238). The important thing for Sethe is that someone has been there to bear witness. This is an example of Sethe's strength and sense of justice.

Sethe tries to tell Denver that she did go back for Halle and gave a woman her children. Sethe has convinced herself she would have recognised Beloved immediately if she had not been distracted by Paul D. The marks on Beloved's head are interpreted as *'fingernail points'* (239).

Sethe dwells on Paul D's criticism; *'Too thick, he said. My love was too thick'* (239). She argues back in her own head that women suffer in particular ways under slavery:

'Would he give his privates to a stranger in return for a carving?' (239).

She is adamant she will protect her family – *'not none of mine'* (239) will have to feel the pain she has felt. She wishes to offer herself to Beloved; *'When I tell you you mine, I also mean I'm yours'* (239). She has not changed her feelings about the death of Beloved or the other attempted murders. Her plan *'was to take us all to the other side'* (240).

She now has a memory of her own mother having the bit and eventually being hanged. Sethe reasons that the bit may have created the 'smile' which she remembers. These traumatic memories are juxtaposed with praise of

Beloved's potential intelligence, as she was a bright baby who *'was crawling already'* (241). She seems soothed by processing her memories, although there is an ominous tone in her assurance that she *'can sleep like the damned'* (241).

Chapter 21 Pages 242-247 *'Beloved is my sister'*

This chapter presents Denver's voice; *'Beloved is my sister'* (242). She remembers hearing Beloved crawl. She also admits she is fearful of Sethe, and that her brothers were frightened of her as well. Denver feels this is the reason that they left for the war. She does not understand Sethe's reasoning and fears she may do it again. Despite her reservations, she realises that real evil *'comes from outside this house...can come right on in the yard if it wants to'* (242). This is the reason Denver never leaves the house. She thinks of her own isolation and remembers her own trauma.

Denver has repressed her memories of the jail, *'a dark place, with scratching noises'* (243). There is evidence of the horror trop when she recalls the sound of *'something little'* in the corner. She feels she has to protect Beloved from Sethe, who *'cut my head off every night'* (243). In a grotesque dream, she cuts the head and braids it.

Denver then repeats the opening description of Baby Suggs's plan for the house. There is an absence in her life. A quiet house *'let me dream my daddy better'* (244). She imagines his fate; she still waits for him. Her alienation is self-imposed as she yearns for a family.

Her memories of her father are vicarious. She relies on Baby Suggs's memories, as she feels *'he was too good for this world'* (245).

Halle had some literacy and numeracy. The story then shifts to the man named after a number (the reader knows him as Sixo). He warns Halle that education may *'make him forget things he shouldn't'* (245).

Denver was the first to guess that the ghost was Beloved. She believes Beloved has come to wait for Halle's return as well. Denver does have the sensitivity to grasp that Baby Suggs was disappointed due to thinking she had control but *'the whitepeople came anyway'* (247).

Baby Suggs told Denver that the ghost would never hurt her. She makes a competing claim for her;

'She's mine, Beloved. She's mine' (247).

Chapter 22 Pages 248-252 *'there is no place where I stop'*

The chapters providing Beloved's perspective are impressionistic in style. After the opening sentence there is no punctuation and there are gaps and silences in the text. She claims one member of the family;

'I am Beloved and she is mine' (248).

Like a developing child, she has no sense of self- *'there is no place where I stop'* (248). She is trying to make sense of the world as she is denied full expression and logic – *'how can I say things that are pictures'*. This can also be read as an allusion to her collective symbolism. She can be all women and all ghosts.

She underlines her timelessness: *'All of it is now'* (248). Her memories are not those of a baby but of a woman exploited by white men, possibly sharing memories of women taken onto the slave ships by *'the men without skin'* (248). The reader must face the horror of *'the little hill of dead people'* (249).

Her memory of a man singing suggests a father, although we know it is not Halle. Likewise, the memory of the mother is not Sethe but a woman who *'goes in the water with my face'*, a reference to the forced suicide from the slave ship. Water divides life and the afterlife as she seems to present a race memory.

Further horrors are suggested when she claims loss of self *'I am going to be in pieces he hurts where I sleep'* (251). The reference to hurt links to a sexual assault, but could be used to support a reading like the earlier interpretation that Beloved has escaped from imprisonment by a male.

Beloved's senses are muddled. She remembers *'chewing and swallowing and laughter'* (251). These comments reflect her dissociation. The diamonds she remembers are both earrings and sparkling water. She fears decay and alienation. There is desolation as she fears 'there is no one to want me'.

Her lack of self is reflected in her desire to fuse with her mother; '*I want th join*' (252). There are repeated references to '*a hot thing*' (252), with it associations with Hell. Beloved is all the ghosts.

Chapter 23 Pages 253-256 '*You are mine*'

This section is a reiteration of Beloved's memories. There is a greater sense of control reflected in the use of punctuation. She expands upon her idea and clarifies. The chapter opens '*I am Beloved and she is mine. Sethe is the one*' (253).

Beloved feels abandoned. She expresses the feelings of the mothers torn from their children in their various homelands and the mothers jumping overboard from the slave ships. She now pictures various maternal figures and sees '*it is my own face smiling*' (254). Beloved's words echo a religious catechism in the question and answer format:

'*...Yes...I was on the other side...*

You rememory me?

Yes. I remember you...' (254).

The text would suggest linked dialogues, from Sethe to Beloved, then Denver to Beloved. Denver would remind Beloved '*Daddy is coming for us*' (255).

Images merge as they move towards the final call and response. Images of milk, smiles and blood merge indicating that family can both nurture and punish.

All three women join in a refrain '*You are mine*' (255). Beloved seem threatening as she commands Sethe '*Don't ever leave me again*' (256). The chapter ends with the repeated affirmation '*You are mine*' (256).

Chapter 24 Pages 257-270 '*His tobacco tin, blown open...*'

Paul D is still living at the Church and has had to process a number of memories; '*His tobacco tin, blown open; spilled contents that floated freely and made him their play and prey*' (258).

He reflects on how he has loved Sethe. He also considers times when he has been helpless, lacking shoes, geography and family.

He has fractured memories of childhood. He feels he has always been alone although he recalls meeting large family networks of ex-slaves. He realises that after the death of Garner *'without his life each of theirs fell to pieces'* (259).

Paul D initially saw Garner as kind for giving them a sense of pride and independence but *'Did a whiteman saying it make it so?'* (260). He can now see that men are emasculated by slavery, silenced by the bit and dehumanised by the three-point collar.

Sethe has shown strength as a mother as well as a woman. Paul D flees her total strength. He sits drinking on the steps of the church. Alcohol does not give him comfort. He recalls the escape plan which was put together by Sixo and the Thirty Mile Woman. The memory is punctuated with a series of 'But' conjunctions. This suggests that fate controls them. Paul *'learns his worth'* (267) as the men in the slavecatching gang discuss him. Sixo was *'woke and laughing'* (269) when they took his life. He admires this bravery and also realises the jeopardy that Sethe may have faced. She was tracked to Cincinnati as she was *'property that reproduced itself without cost'* (269). He ends his recollection that the rooster was smiling.

Chapter 25 Pages 271-280 *'All he can'*

Stamp Paid finds Paul D to apologise. Paul D reassures him that the preacher did offer him a room but he chose to stay in the church cellar. The interaction demonstrates how men have struggled to process the emotions generated by the evils of slavery. Paul D seems to fear claiming his own humanity.

Stamp Paid relates the story of his wife Vashti. This is a fuller version than his earlier recollection, another example of reiteration and the 'rememory' that forms a theme of the novel. He remembers the urge to break her neck when the master tired of her and 'returned' her. Here he draws a link between his own uncontrollable feelings and the protective instinct which drove Sethe to kill Beloved.

He tries to encourage empathy with Sethe and shares what he witnessed the day she killed Beloved. Both men share their fear and mistrust of Beloved.

Like Ella, Stamp Paid considers her to be a human trickster, perhaps an unfortunate who was trapped in a house. When the image of her being trapped there since childhood or 'a pup' is presented Paul D counters *'Well, now she's a bitch'* (277). The stark animal imagery recalls his rebuke towards Sethe after her confession. Paul D feels he cannot take any more and questions the need for suffering, but Stamp Paid encourages him to take *'All he can'* (277).

3.4 Part III: Chapters 26-28 *'Although she has claim, she is not claimed'*

In this section we will;

- *Consider how language and imagery convey writer's intentions in Beloved*
- *Evaluate the methods employed by Morrison to convey the patterns of natural speech and thought processes*
- *To show understanding of how Morrison's choice of form, structure and language shapes meanings.*

Chapter 26 Pages 281-309 *'124 was quiet'*

The third and final section presents the denouement of the story. It opens *'124 was quiet'* (281). Sethe has seen the handsaw scar on Beloved's neck and commits to atoning for her actions in any way that is required. Sethe seeks forgiveness from Beloved, who repeats that she has abandoned her. Beloved would have them all unite *'on the other side, forever'*.

Sethe is starved in the house, having spent her savings on ribbons and dresses, luxuries and trinkets bought to amuse Beloved. Denver realises the situation has become drastic. She knows she has to get help and so prepares *'to step off the edge of the world and die'* (281).

There is an unnatural symbiosis. As Beloved is *'getting bigger, plumper by the day'* (281) while Sethe's clothes sag. Beloved may be pregnant as a result of being with Paul D. Beloved and Sethe exclude Denver, and the situation worsens when Sethe loses her job. Denver recalls the time they spend playing and sewing. They engage in a fantasy world; *'the three of them looked like carnival women with nothing to do'* (283).

Beloved seems now to have everything she wanted and when things ran out *'Beloved invented desire'* (283). In the arguments that followed Sethe cried while Beloved became angry.

Beloved speaks of her own ghosts who *'said beloved in the dark and bitch in the light'* (284). Denver realises that she was not like them – *'She was wild game...'* (285). Denver tries to help. She is perplexed that Sethe seems to ignore Beloved's *'basket-fat stomach'* (285).

Denver realises that that the family dynamic is corrupt; all three are *'locked in a love that wore everybody out'* (286). Denver sees the need to protect Sethe from Beloved. In going for help she confronts her real fear of *'out there'* (287).

At this point Denver remembers Sethe and Baby Suggs disagreeing about whether there are any helpful white people. Baby Suggs had concluded *'There's more if us they drowned than there is all of them ever lived from the start of time'* (287).

It's the imagined voice of Baby Suggs that eventually prompts Denver to go out into the world. Vague memories of the town begin to flood back as she makes her way to Lady Jones. The details on Lady Jones reveals problems faced by mixed race women and provides an example of racism created by slavery. From mixed race parentage, she herself was ostracised as being *'yellow'* and *'white'* (291). She also has a low sense of self, hating her own image, particularly her hair, 'every strand of which she hated'.

Denver shares her mother's pride. She doesn't want charity but is thankful when food starts to appear. The names left on each encourage her to go out and connect with the community. She is welcomed as *'they were sorry for the years of their own disdain'* (293).

Denver returns to her lessons with Lady Jane and learns some Bible verses. This is in direct opposition to the hellish picture in 124; *'...the women had arrived at a doomsday truce designed by the devil'* (294).

Beloved curls up on the floor and self-harms. Sethe is diminished by Beloved's constant demands; *'She sat in the chair licking her lips like a chastised child while Beloved ate up her life, took it, swelled up with it, grew taller on it'* (295).

Denver is now looking after them both. She has become the bridge between past and future. She has started to develop an independent self and is building links between Sethe and the community.

Sethe is unresponsive, driven by fear that Beloved might leave. She had believed the worst fate was that once faced by Baby Suggs; *'That anybody white could take your whole self for anything that came to mind'* (295). Sethe once again considers the myriad ways in which slavery could debase and destroy a person. Owners would *'Not just work, kill, or maim you, but dirty you'* (295).

This immediately triggers her urge to protect her children; *'The best thing she was, was her children'* (296). She has worked to keep her daughters away from the horrors of slavery. She would not have them listed *'on the animal side of the paper'* (296). Sethe has sustained mental and spiritual wounds relating to her own abuse and her decision to kill her child. Sethe demonstrates how destructive it can be to base life around the past.

Beloved embodies the haunting legacy of slavery. She prevents Sethe and Denver from moving on with their lives.

Denver, like Halle, has to hire herself out. Nelson Lord now speaks to her and the gradual reintegration into the community has *'opened her mind'* (297). She arranges to work for the Bodwins. While there she confides in current servant Janey Wagon. Denver as a free woman is aware of the legacy of slavery. She is troubled by the figurine of the young black boy claiming to be *'At Yo' Service'* (300).

The story of 124 begins to spread through gossip and it is clear that most believe Beloved is a revenant and supernatural in nature. They all believe *'It's back'* (301). While some women donate food, others are moved to action.

At this point, a little of Ella's history is provided. She feels she can understand Sethe's rage but found her reasoning *'prideful'* (302). However, she will show solidarity with Sethe to fight an *'invasion'* (302) from another world.

The women gather, bringing talismans, tokens and Christian relics. Lady Jones does not participate as she sees the superstition as ignorance. The action builds to a climax as Denver waits for Bodwin to collect her for work. It is symbolic that the women gather at *'three in the afternoon on a Friday'* (302). This recalls Christ's crucifixion. It is an ambiguous image, as it suggests suffering and sacrifice and perhaps aligns Beloved with angels rather than demons.

As Sethe has done throughout the novel, the women of the town have to revisit their memories of the past, often referencing the party at 124. Realising their part in Sethe's downfall a number of them kneel and pray.

There is a realisation that a new approach must be taken. It is perhaps ironic that to do so they must look to an ancient past;

'In the beginning there were no words. In the beginning was the sound' (305).

Parallel to this, there is a narrative jump to Bodwin making his way towards 124 to pick up Denver for work. Bodwin visits his own memories of the house, revealing that several of his own female relatives had dies there. He also buried his childhood treasures there. Like Lady Jones, he occupies the position of the outsider. His abolitionist views and practical support of the black community earn him the epithet of *'bleached nigger'* (309).

He recalls trying to help Sethe. Sethe is holding an ice pick, which briefly foreshadows the ensuing action. She has been drawn outside by the voices and *'she trembled like the baptized in its wash'* (308). In comparison to her weakened state the witnesses view the pregnant Beloved as *'dazzling'* (308).

It is at this point Sethe confuses Bodwin's wide-brimmed hat with that of schoolteacher. There is a repetition and echo of earlier images as Sethe recalls the *'little hummingbirds'* (309).

It is noted that *'Beloved is smiling'* (309) as she sees her mother defending her. The violence here leads to Sethe's reintegration. As the novel switches to Beloved's point of view she sees her mother defend her but confuses the women for the pile of bodies on the slave ship. She disappears in the exorcism. It may be argued that the whole novel is an exorcism.

Chapter 27 Pages 310-322 *'You your best thing…'*

The chapter begins with Paul D's song. There is a sense of renewed hope. Here Boy has returned so Paul D seems sure that Beloved is *'truly gone'* (310). There is a final reference to the supernatural as witnesses claim Beloved *'exploded right before their eyes'* (310).

Paul D has time to reflect on the events at 124. He has shame at the *'brainless urge'* (311) of his encounters with Beloved. Bodwin is planning to sell 124. While this will allow a new start, it is an example of how even well-meaning white abolitionists can exert power and change the fate of others.

The tone has changed to a more light-hearted and optimistic one as Paul D and Stamp Paid can laugh at *'crazy'* (312) Sethe. Stamp Paid defends Denver saying *'That's my heart'* (313). He explains how she sought help. He meets a more confident Denver, who has maintained two jobs and is training to be a teacher. Denver does issue a challenge to Paul D in reference to Beloved.

The town have claimed they have seen her go to the water. Beloved is once again linked with water imagery, as she was when she first appeared. Paul D remembers being powerless in the cold house. He felt drowned, *'beached and gobbling air'* as though he was back from *'some ocean deep place he once belonged to'*. As with Denver, he seems to have experienced a trauma from further back in history.

While he does not fully understand, he links his coupling with Beloved with a type of re-birth; from this moment he feels he can process memories.

Paul D recounts being on both sides during the war, beginning with the Union before *'slave-working'* for the Rebels sorting the dead. He has managed five escapes in his life and the hardest thing of all is that *'he could not help being astonished by the beauty of this land that was not his'* (316).

In returning to the house he notices there is no trace of the red and aggressive presence. In its place there is now *'a bleak and minus nothing. More like absence'* (318).

Sethe is in anguish; she remains under a quilt humming a lullaby. Sethe is dangerously close to death. She still dwells on the ink she made and claims to be tired of life like Baby Suggs.

Paul D once again has the power to make women to cry in from of him. He is weary but grateful to be with Sethe, who releases her emotions in front of him. She is bereft that Beloved has left her; *'She was my best thing'* (321).

Paul D remembers Sixo's woman was *'a woman who is a friend of your mind'* (321). He realises that he may have a future with Sethe if he can help her discover her sense of self, and knows 'He wants to put his story next to hers' (322).

Paul D encourages Sethe and dismisses her insecurities. He assures her *'You your best thing, Sethe'* (322). The text ends with a repeated question, *'Me? Me?'* (322), the second question suggesting an emerging sense of self.

Chapter 28 Pages 323-324 *'This is not a story to pass on'*

The final two pages present an epilogue and suggest a peaceful conclusion Its message is ambiguous. It begins by referencing the *'loneliness that can be rocked'* (323) which challenges the loneliness that starves; *'It is alive, on its own'* (323).

The text suggests Beloved has been gradually forgotten, *'Disremembered and unaccounted for'* (323). While she was disruptive, she had an important message about the importance of memory, particularly when we are asked to remember the forgotten. There is a note of sympathy as it is observed *'Although she has claim, she is not claimed'* (323).

> **Task: Ambiguity in the novel**
>
> The key ambiguity turns on the repeated iteration *'It was not a story to pass on'*.
>
> To what extent does the ending ask the reader to forget?
>
> What should be remembered?

Initially the community work hard to place the trouble behind them – *'Remembering seemed unwise'* (324). However, the subtle shift in the instruction *'This is not a story to pass on'* suggests the opposite of forgetting. It asks that we do not ignore the ghosts and dispossessed.

There is the suggestion that Beloved is a force or presence necessary in the world, and there are hints she remains, in *'knuckles brushing a cheek in sleep'* (324) and footprints by the stream near 124. Sethe and Denver note that the natural world and seasons have eventually reclaimed power. Beloved has returned to the creek, a symbol of the flow of life and time.

The text ends on a single word. It can be an epitaph to a dead girl, a call to all those who feel disowned or a command to remind all to accept love and community; *'Beloved'* (324).

Part Four:
Contexts of Reception

4.1 Critical Reception: Contemporary Reviews
4.2 Critical Contexts and Approaches: Genre-Based and Structuralist Approaches
4.3 Critical Contexts and Approaches: Psychoanalytical and Gendered Readings
4.4 Critical Contexts and Approaches: Historicist and Post-Colonial Readings

4.1 Critical Reception: Contemporary Reviews

n this section we will;

- *Demonstrate understanding of the significance and influence of the contexts in which literary texts are written and received*
- *Explore connections across literary texts and contexts*
- *To show understanding of how Morrison's choice of form, structure and language shapes meanings.*

Contexts of Reception: Critical Responses and Linking Texts

As well as appreciating the **historical contexts** of the novel presented in **Part One: Contexts of Production**, you will be expected to develop an understanding of how readers have received the novel. This can be in a range of contexts. It can be useful to consider how readers at the time reacted to the narrative and its presentation of childhood. Where this information is hard to come by, it can be illuminating to consider how the writer was viewed at the time of writing and this forms part of the reading activity later in this section.

Another form of reception is **critical reception**. This involves exploration of academic responses to the text, usually written by researchers with a literary background. This is good preparation for higher level undergraduate study and can also serve to provide new perspectives on the text which you may not have considered.

Last but by no means least, you must learn to value your own **response as a reader**. Barthes argued for the 'death of the author'. A text will only mean what the reader wants it to mean. The examination will encourage you to present your own interpretations of the presentation of particular themes linked to the idea of childhood.

Separatist vs. Syncretist Approaches

Critical theory would introduce a politics of reading which would question where should the text sit, within a Western or African-American cultural tradition? A number of critics approach the text with caution, fearing appropriation of the text. This has been dealt with in a number of ways. Catherine Belsey sees *Beloved* as the transformation of a love story and sees the mother-daughter relationship as central and universal. Gayatri Spivak encourages readers to accept their own reading position but to read across gender and racial differences to consider shifts in perception.

Linden Peach notes that critical responses can often be categorised as:

❖ Separatist and
❖ Syncretist.

Separatists place the text in an African-American context, noting the potential use of Western theoretical frames such as psychoanalytical, Marxist and feminist readings, but also argue that these do not fully engage with the African traditions and forms present in the novel.

There is a debate surrounding the claims for a separatist literature. Often the debate centres on the 'black aesthetic'. The selected texts can be seen to have a role in countering negative stereotypes and presenting black consciousness.

Syncretists find it more productive to view the novel as a culturally hybrid form. For example, it has been proposed that the text combines the female Gothic with conventions of the slave narrative.

Some readers compare Morrison's work to the Western tradition of writers such as Faulkner and Woolf due to the fragmentation of time in her works. Morrison rejects this approach as 'it never goes into the work on its own terms' (p.122, *Black Women Writers* Ed. Claudia Tata, New York, Continuum, 1984).

A key argument against liberal humanist approaches which place *Beloved* in the classical literary tradition is that these are based around concepts of self, identity and individuality which sit in some opposition to the affirmation of African-American community. Additionally, liberal humanism privileges certain groups over an imagined 'Other'. Concepts are presented based on cultural and gender-specific assumptions.

TASK: Exploring Contemporary Reviews

The New York Times columnist Michiko Kakutani wrote that Beloved

'possesses the heightened power and resonance of myth – its characters, like those in an opera or Greek drama, seem larger than life and their actions, too, tend to strike us as enactments of ancient rituals and passions. To describe Beloved only in these terms, however, is to diminish its immediacy, for the novel also remains precisely grounded in American reality – the reality of black history as experienced in the wake of the civil war.'

The extract above was published in *The New York Times* in 1987.

Which elements of Morrison's writing style have been praised?
Can you think of examples of 'myth' in the novel?
Can you think of examples of 'the reality of black history' in the novel?

Critical Reception: Early Reviews

> *Beloved* has been placed in a wider cultural context. Early responses often engaged with ideas of canonicity.

A S Byatt 'An American Masterpiece' *The Guardian.* 16ᵗʰ October 1987

This review notes the key issues of motherhood, memory and role of language as way of dominating in context of slavery. Byatt also questions Beloved's relation to American literature and culture.

> Beloved represents pain and suffering. This is epitomised by mother love which resorts to murder due to the torture of slavery. The text is 'no thin allegory or shrill tract'.

> Naming also features in the discussion. Byatt notes 'their names are the no-names of non-people'. Characters are seen as resembling fairytale heroes. Byatt compares Morrison to Tolstoy, as 'the reader is inside in their doings and sufferings'.

> Throughout the novel, she notes the distanced world of whites. The emotional repression shown is the 'deliberate limitation of memory' (17). Morrison makes use of the animal imagery often employed by the scientific rationalists but goes on to 'present an image of a people so wholly human that they are almost superhuman' (17).

Byatt judges the novel as 'an American masterpiece' (18). Melville Hawthorne and Poe presented allegories on evil, unappeased spirits opposition of blackness and whiteness. Morrison has 'solved the riddle, and showed us the world which haunted theirs' (18). It is interesting that Morrison herself went on to argue that the American canon presents mediated responses to the presence of the black population. Presence is notable even in absence.

Thomas R Edwards 'Ghost Story' from *New York Review of Books*. 5 November 1987.

Edwards recognises the demands of the text. This novel 'goes back into history, and behind history into the materials of myth and fantasy'. The novel for Edwards proposes to be a ghost story about slavery. Unlike the scepticism in Dickens, Collins and James, here the reader must accept the ghost.

Edwards examines Beloved's physicality, deciding 'this is the grotesque comedy of certain moods of folklore, in which figures of extra-human potency and menace are partly humanized by assuming some of our own vulnerability'. Beloved seems familiar and this is what makes her so dangerous. Edwards acknowledges that there is a difficulty in invoking the Gothic tradition, which would support an ethnocentrism which would obscure elements specific to African-American folk culture.

An alternative was proposed by Barbara Christian who argued that Beloved as an embodied spirit reflected traditional African ancestor worship. Beloved is then 'a sign of a continually developing African cosmology'.

For Edwards the novel is primarily a book about survival and memory. He suggests that 'None of Morrison's people have entire access to the truth'. Beloved has an impossible desire and hopes to merge with mother. This has an element of folklore and her impossible wish will lead to catastrophe. The resolution produces a response to the original tragedy as Sethe fights the invader rather than turn on her child.

There is a central paradox in the relationship between memory and history. We wish to still be part of something we now understand and perhaps find fault with. Memory isolated from life can be dangerous. Beloved is 'all memory'.

Like a number of critics, Edwards attempts to tease out the paradox of the final pages – this is a story that should not be told but must be told. The memory of social horrors distorts life, yet living without any regard to memory is trivial. It is hoped that the novel may support the thoughtful female black reader to 'recreate an imagination of self'. Edwards here does not feel he is equipped to fully dissect the text as a white male reader not at the centre of the narrative. Nevertheless, he deems this a powerful and important text with claim to the canon.

Stanley Crouch 'Aunt Medea' *New Republic.* 19th October 1987

> It can be illuminating to examine the arguments presented by those critical of the work. One critique engaged with by Morrison herself was the vitriolic attack on the text soon after its publication by Stanley Crouch. He accused the novel of being sentimental and felt Morrison's work is tied more closely to a European literary tradition rather than an African-American one.

Crouch begins by grouping Morrison with Alice Walker, claiming both women present a vision of suffering as a source of liberation and enlightenment for all readers. Walker had seen success a few years earlier with her novel *The Color Purple.* He groups both women within a wider feminist ideology reaching back into the 1970s. He claims it is glib and divisive, based on a criticism of patriarchal oppression, even from black males. Crouch labels Morrison as 'dangerously feminist'.

It has been noted that Crouch has made errors in his review, calling *Beloved* Morrison's fourth novel when it was in fact her fifth published prose work. He seems scathing of the narrative, feeling it is underpinned by a feminist approach which sets out 'to make sure that the vision of black woman as the most scorned and rebuked of victims doesn't weaken'.

His most shocking attack is when he argues that Morrison's reference to the 'Sixty Million and more' potentially lost in the Middle Passage is an attempt to claim a holocaust in a 'big-time martyr ratings contest' (26). He is quick to clarify that he is not criticising the collective tragedy of the lives lost due to the slave trade but merely Morrison's style which he feels 'lacks a true sense of the tragic'.

Crouch continues to recognise that Morrison has skills as a writer, drawing attention to her motifs, but complains that 'she perpetually interrupts her narrative with maudlin ideological commercials' (27). He identifies first-class writing in the characterisation of Stamp Paid and Lady Jones, finding them 'superbly drawn'. He also gives examples of simple descriptive passages which he feels are the text's strength.

Crouch reads the text as a melodrama with characters fates already determined. It is this context which leads him to cast Sethe as 'Aunt Medea'. He feels Morrison loses control of her writing, unable to 'resist the temptation of the trite or sentimental'.

He examines the passage where the women come to exorcise Beloved and he feels Morrison's inclusion of Biblical allusions and folk rhythms here 'stymie a book that might have been important'.

Other critics point out that much of Crouch's negativity is a projection of personal and cultural anxieties. Crouch seems to want a humanism that Morrison sees as part of problem. It could even be suggested that an examination of slavery and the Holocaust together would provide a useful discussion on how humanism and rational science has been abused by those in power.

Other Literary Reviews

A number of reviews centre around the ambiguity of Beloved herself. Phelan sees her as textually 'stubborn' and ambiguous in what she is supposed to represent. As with Edwards, there is a reluctance to critically engage as a white male reading the text.

TASK: Critical Reviews

To what extent would you support each interpretation of *Beloved*?

You should consider:
- Language and imagery used to describe Beloved and her actions
- How other characters respond to Beloved
- Presentation of themes in the novel

Making Silence Speak: Toni Morrison and the Beloved Community of Memory

Critical Reading: Brendese, P. (2014) 'Making Silence Speak: Toni Morrison and the Beloved Community '

Morrison has noted the core problem of first hand slavery accounts as documentary. Given that these texts were often produced to encourage support for abolitionists, with the possibility of a general and genteel female readership, ex-slaves were often unable to present the most gruesome and dehumanising elements of their treatment. In creating a fictional account of the trials facing one woman, Morrison began a process of 'moving the veil aside'. This fictional intervention aims to give a voice to a previously muted history. Morrison 'passes on' previous versions of history yet the novel does not end in a clear affirmation, rather presenting a challenge to readers to remember.

In the novel 'Beloved makes silence speak'. She encourages memory and reflection, with the story ending with a form of acceptance and looking towards the future. There is a difficulty in accepting a happy ending. If we read the removal of Beloved as the past being redeemed by the present, the readers become complicit, 'by assuming closure they participate in the very amnesia the book critiques' (Brendese, 2014). Alternatively, the ending can be read as a 'tragic irresolution' – Sethe has returned to a beloved community but they remain haunted by memories and the ghosts they have repressed. Morrison uses her imagination to explore the idea of inherited silences which oppress future generations.

In the real-life case of Margaret Garner the abolitionists wanted her tried for murder as only a person can be accused of this crime and to do so would show she was more than a piece of property. Some readers argue that Sethe may have escaped but has traded slavery for 'a life of servitude to a past that returns unbidden'.

Sethe begins by reflecting there was 'nothing to tell except Schoolteacher'. He has written her history and shaped her life. Sethe cannot remove her feeling of complicity with his project due to her part in making the ink which recorded her traits.

Beloved emerges from the water under the bridge. She arrives at the exact point when Sethe feels she can leave things in the past, having had a day out at the carnival with Denver and Paul D. Beloved arrives with an appetite for sugary foods and stories. These stories provoke 're-memory', unconscious memories which emerge and need to be engaged with. Until this point Sethe has her past by not engaging with it.

Some critics have gone further in their exploration of Beloved as antagonist. Not only does she make Sethe deal with uncomfortable memories but 'Beloved's characteristics as a lazy, junk-food eating, over-dressed, inarticulate, libidinous, self-interested parasite directly mirror the recurring stigma of African-Americans', powered by 'unconscious connections to the past'. A more sympathetic view would argue that Beloved cannot have peaceful rest due to the violence of her short life. The solution seems to be to the ability to both look ahead but also respect the debt to previous suffering.

Sethe is not able to achieve this by herself. She needs the community to aid in Beloved's exorcism. The novel also seems to stress the importance of oral histories and shared experience. Amy Denver and Sethe literally find themselves 'in the same boat' during the labour and support each other as runaways.

Innocence seems to have been lost, whether it is Bodwin's watch and toy soldiers which form part of the childhood treasure buried at 124, or Sethe's earrings which symbolise a token of affection from Mrs Garner. The earrings had reminded her that some white people could be helpful. Now buried,

Sethe confuses the abolitionist Bodwin with the schoolteacher and lunges for him in error when the women come to dispel Beloved.

The ending of the novel remains ambiguous. It suggests that following the disappearance of Beloved there is a shared bliss in forgetting and some move forward. However, there are traces of her and the reader is instructed not to pass on or forget. The novel has lingered on images stuck in the memory yet warns the reader not to linger on a photo. This is perhaps a comment on disavowal and reconciliation. There is a sense of 'active forgetting'. However, if they forget the ghost, they will forget something once 'beloved'; 'The community cannot claim its identity without claiming its slave past, but it refuses' (86).

The final word of the text is 'Beloved'. This may suggest future ghosts but also has some hope that there will be a community of memory to start to reclaim the excluded, forgotten and unloved.

SELLING A MOTHER FROM HER CHILD.

" 'Do you *often* buy the wife without the husband ?' 'Yes, *very often ;* and *frequently,* too, they sell me the mother while they keep her children. I have often known them take away the infant from its mother's breast, and keep it, while they sold her.' "—*Prof. Andrews, late of the University of N. C., in his recent work on Slavery and the Slave-Trade, p.* 147, *relates the foregoing conversation with a slave-trader on the Potomac.*

Morrison passes on or conveys a story not to be passed on, or refused. The story does expose the myth of the happy ending. Slavery has not 'passed on' as the legacy of the trauma is what has been passed on or inherited. It has also been suggested that the community wilfully forgetting the events with Beloved is a parody of America's pretence at harmony or the idea of segregated memory. This is still evident in recent objections to a museum in Alabama commemorating the victims of lynching.

There remains a difficulty in equating memory with democracy as this can suggest a moral equivalence between the oppressor and the oppressed. There remains a lack of comprehension regarding the ways in which supremacist Reconstructionist policies contributed to segregation which influences American History lessons today. There is still a reluctance to use the past to view present conflicts. Some critics suggest that Morrison's novel can be viewed as part of a wider message. That until racism is viewed as part of history, we cannot understand its role in creating modern inequalities. In the novel Morrison creates a 'politics of memory'.

4.2 Genre-Based and Post-Structuralist Approaches

In this section we will;
- *Demonstrate understanding of the significance and influence of the contexts in which literary texts are written and received*
- *Explore connections across literary texts and contexts*
- *To show understanding of how Morrison's choice of form, structure and language shapes meanings.*

Critical Reception: Academic Sources

Let us now turn our attention to literary criticism. A-Level and IB Literature students may already familiar with this type of text from work on other units. When working independently with texts, as you will for this unit, you may encounter critical readings intended for undergraduate and postgraduate readers. They can be quite daunting but with a bit of exposure to these types of texts, you will gain confidence and should be able to draw on the information presented in them to present original ideas about your literature texts. Throughout this section, the details of the sources of further critical discussion are provided and these can provide you with extended learning opportunities.

Early Critical Reception

Criticism from the 1970s and 1980s placed emphasis on the ways in which white American culture dominated African-American communities.

In the 1980s African-American criticism shifted from race to look at gender. Toni Morrison stressed the ways in which race, gender and class were inter related. There was a focus on feminist cultural politics, including identification of race-specific responses to the patriarchy. White female critics showed awareness that they held positions in the racist patriarchal order which formed the status quo. There was an intellectual renaissance in the later decades of the twentieth century, with political as well as literary interventions.

Feminist Readings

Barbara Rigney presents a feminist deconstruction highlighting that self and race are not meaningful or stable categories. Morrison's writing reformulates self, identity and history, creating a 'multiplicity of the self'. Concepts of autonomy and closer are not always useful as African-American model is based on a 'sense of diffusion and fragmentation' (11). Morrison' maternal space is one of danger as well as desire. In *Beloved* the daughter is the primary aggressor and there is anxiety about and even fear of maternal aggression.

Critics apply aspects of French feminism – typified by Julia Kristeva and Helene Cixous -to acknowledge the way names are allied to a culture and history rather than being individual. There is ambiguity in matriarchal and maternal power. Throughout the novel there is a merging of characters with the identity of the community.

Rigney argues that at times Morrison romanticises the African past and employs the myth of the African Great Mother as an ideal figure of redemption, yet presents an ironic qualification of a lost Africa.

Payant feels Morrison includes 'linguistic disorder which is truly feminine'. An uneasy alliance is stressed between men and women, united by the common experience of white oppression. Their abuse of often explained by the way men have been emotionally and sexually crippled by racism. Morrison also acknowledges wrong-doing of women.

Marxist Readings

Cynthia Davis looked at how Morrison represented the problem of maintaining cultural heritage under psychological and environmental stress. This could be regarded as a Marxist sociological perspective. Davis examines the shift in meaning of myth towards an ideology. She warns of the dangers of removing myth from the black context. Morrison combines aspects of myth with concrete situations of oppression. Davis argues that Morrison re-writes Western classical myth. Readers such as Payant accused Morrison of limiting her female characters, suggesting that myth out of context will simplify history. The appropriateness of European critical interpretations of myths is questioned. In the novel, Morrison sees a 'fall' as a necessary gesture for freedom.

The central tenet of Marxism is that the social being determines consciousness. We are 'constructed' by society in which we are born and in which we live. Literature is a product of society but can also shape society. Mbalia admires Morrison's 'people-class perspective'. There is a continued focus on highlighting exploitation and oppression.

Structuralism

The terms structuralism and post-structuralism suggest architecture. It can be a useful metaphor for literature and the examination of texts. Deconstruction suggests a lack of clear boundaries and gaps.

Structuralist reading

Critical
Reading:
Krumholz, L.
'The Ghosts
of Slavery:
Historical
Recovery in
Toni
Morrison's
Beloved'.
*African
American
Review* Vol.
26, No. 3
(Autumn,
1992).

In *Beloved*, there is a focus on modernist techniques such as the fragmentation of plot and shift in narrative voice. The reader reconstruction of fragments parallels Sethe's recovery. The text also make use of oral techniques such as repetition, the blending of voices, shifts perspective and the episodic framework.

The three phases of the text present a reckoning of the history of slavery ar echo the three stages of the healing process:

❖ Repression of memories and the trauma of slavery
❖ Painful reconciliation
❖ A clearing and 're-birth' of the sufferer.

Part I presents stories through fragmented recollections, as it is revealed that Sethe murdered a child.

Part II includes voices of despair. The ritual chants of Sethe, Denver an Beloved dominate as well as the memories of Stamp Paid and Paul D. Wh. is revealed is the legacy of slavery.

Part III could be regarded as the reader's 'clearing'. There is brief comic reli in the reflections of Paul D and Stamp Paid. After the exorcism there is hope of reunion between Sethe and Paul D as they plan for the future.

While the novel becomes 'a ritual of healing' after the disruption and uneas embodied in Beloved, it is also true that while an eruption she proves to b a catalyst for healing. Krumholz finds her to be a 'trickster' figure. The ghos of Beloved and Baby Suggs stir the healing process.

Krumholz argues that Morrison constructs the African-American psych using Western literature and philosophy as models, creating an overt Freudian narrative. The metaphorical space of the Clearing merges Africai American ritual with Christian symbolism.

Morrison sets out to reconstruct the past in order to reshape the future. Th text is history-making. In Morrison, morality is not black and white. Methoc used may be judged as good and evil. The only moral or evil absolute wou seem to be in the character of 'schoolteacher'. He embodies the wror methods. He aims to educate in 'facts' and imposes the category of slav upon Sethe.

Beloved would seem to embody the repressed past. While she is Sethe ghost, she also forces Paul D to confront his shame and powerlessness, ar forces Denver to deal with her mother's history as a slave.

The reader must realise that the historic past can create a living vindictive present. Beloved can represent suffering and guilt but also be powerful and beautiful. The final image of her is 'pregnant with possibilities'. Her final appearance is both the 'African mother' and also consuming devil child.

The importance of 'writing' in *Beloved*

Durkin's key thesis highlights that while the novel is rightfully analysed in terms of the ways in which it relates to oral traditions, there is still relatively less focus on the place of writing in the narrative. Durkin argues that this 'seems to indicate writing as a central theme in Beloved'.

While Sethe does not write, Morrison repeatedly refers to inscribed bodies. Durkin argues that Morrison emphasises the ways in which slaves are textual bodies and are written on in various ways. This can often be disturbing, as evidenced in the scars which write the history of enslavement on their bodies; '*In scarring, the human body thus becomes the site of writing*' (Durkin, 2007).

Critical Reading:
Durkin, A. 'Object Written, Written Object: Slavery, Scarring, and Complications of Authorship in Beloved'. *African American Review*. Vol. 41, No. 3 (2006).

Sethe links her 'branches' back to the ink used to list her animal traits. There is an inextricable link between scarring and writing. A duality exists in the text between oral and written, enslavement and freedom. Sethe dwells on the fact that she made the ink that is used to chart her 'animal' characteristics. She sees herself as complicit in her own subjugation. Ultimately, a white man has had power over her story when she was at Sweet Home. In the exploitation of Sethe's milk, the violent animalism of the nephews is ignored as Sethe is forced into the caricature of the 'Mammy'. The attack on her body is a further perversion of the wet nurses, the black women forced to nurse the white children of the plantation owners at the expense of their own children's health. Schoolteacher observes and takes notes as the young men assault her and take her milk.

Durkin notes that theatre practitioner Brooks references the significance of scars as a way of signifying and identifying individuals in classical Greek tragedy and Homer's *Odyssey*. Morrison herself studied Greek tragedy and felt it was a genre which provided an intellectual home. She drew similarities between classical Greek social structures.

In slavery, the mark is the identity of the slave. It is an imposed identity – '*both a signifier of identity and the construction of identity*' (Durkin, 2007). These marks also create white identity, as labelling the 'other' identifies the self. Throughout the body is read as a text. Sethe's 'tree' can also become a family tree, linking her to the 'sixty million and more' who may have perished on the route to slavery. While this is a reminder of tragic and enormous loss, there can be some positive elements as *'the scar acts as an emblem of community and connection'* (Durkin, 2007). In this way it could be argued that the scar is no longer under slaveowner's control.

There is a possibility that when readers focus on the oral patterns, metafiction and intertextuality can be ignored. Morrison's novel does raise questions about the American literary canon and Eurocentric and white perspectives. The themes echo debates presented by Morrison in her critical non-fiction.

Morrison herself suggests that white American writers cannot help but construct works and aesthetics *'through the uncertainties of racial identification'*.

Morrison sees the literary canon as political. Narratives are often used to solidify white identity. The canon is built on exclusion. Texts often operate on a dichotomy. Whiteness is often defined by oppositional differentiation to the black population. Morrison politically terms this a literary 'miscegenation' – writers need 'blackness' to define 'whiteness'.

Traditional American novels create tensions for the black writer. They are using a medium which would position African- Americans and indigenous populations as blanks, absences or oppositional forces. African-Americans become 'ghosts'. Morrison takes these ghosts and returns them in the presence of Beloved.

Can the written novel truly present experience or convey oral tradition?

Morrison makes use of both geographic and domestic settings, as well as the space created by the novel itself. There is a focus on structure, language and the text as object. The novel challenges the 'absence' in traditional texts. In presenting this challenge, it may be that traditional and canonical theoretical positions may not be sufficient tools of analysis.

While it is true that the text shares some conventional features of the oral tradition, it does remain a novel. The text has *'simultaneity of orality and writing'*.

Morrison in turn overwrites Margaret Garner's story, omitting any suggestion that the child is a product of rape by the plantation owner, as well as the emphasis placed on Garner's own mixed parentage and pale skin. In doing so, she keeps the focus on black experience, with Sethe's baby a symbol of purity who must be saved from the taint of slavery. In this way the novel does correspond with oral tradition, which relies on the multiple re-tellings of known narratives;

'Read through Morrison's employment of orality in *Beloved*, the over-writing of narrative appears as a retelling of white narratives that is some sense is also a revision of white narratives. This could be regarded as akin to Derrida's idea of the 'supplement'. The story stands in relation to the traditional canon. The re-telling is also evident as Beloved assumed other characters' identities at various points in the story. Baby Suggs attempts to re-interpret bodies and identities in her community preaching.

It could be argued that Sethe sets herself up in 124 in opposition to the community. Sethe lacks a coherent sense of self until she addresses her memories and trauma. Only then can she re-join the community.

In telling her story Sethe is both subject and object of narrative. This is traumatic in itself as becoming an object reminds her of being a slave. There is an overlap in identities. This is not always negative. At the end of the novel, Paul D offers to put his story alongside hers. At the end there is a sense that Sethe is reclaiming herself '*Me?Me?*' as subject and object of a more positive future.

It can be argued that in wanting to possess Sethe completely, Beloved enacts violence against her. Likewise, Sethe's attempts to kill her children marks them. This is in a different way to the slaveowners, acting as signs that they are not slaves. Later in the novel, Sethe tries to kill Bodwin, mistaking him for the schoolteacher. Rather than turn on her children, in the second encounter she tries to erase white men from her story.

While a number of critics have noted the marginal status of white characters in the novel, Durkin argues whites and issues of ownership are a constant presence in the novel. Even in the Clearing, rules prevent Sethe from burying Baby Suggs where she loved to preach. Baby Suggs seems to deteriorate and die following the shock that slave catchers came into her yard. Denver spends her life uncertain on how to 'tell' about white people.

The novel ends with a degree of ambiguity. In insisting it is a story 'not to pass on' there is a sense that it may be a story not to repeat. Conversely, this phrase could also press the reader not to overlook or forget what they have read. The phrase is repeated, with a subtle change from 'It' to 'This', directly asking the reader to reflect on the message of the novel itself. Durkin presents this as a 'confluence of writing and orality' (Durkin, 2007).

The novel itself can be seen as a site for the difficult negotiation between respecting the oral narratives of the African-American tradition whilst working in the written medium of the novel, which has been shaped by dominant ideologies. In the case of *Beloved*, it writes back to American writers such as Mark Twain and Herman Melville, who are writing from a position of power.

Durkin (2007) concludes by arguing not enough critical attention has be[en] paid to the 'obsession with writing and with written bodies' in the no[vel] *Beloved* is seen as transcribing its own complex heritage.

Beloved and the Supernatural

Morrison seeks to recognise the supernatural and magic as 'another way [of] knowing things'. These belief systems may have been discredited in mode[rn] society but in *Beloved* she seeks to present characters who 'blend t[he] acceptance of the supernatural and a profound rootedness in the real wo[rld] at the same time with neither taking the precedence over the other' (['] from Toni Morrison 'Rootedness: The Ancestor as Foundation' in Vl[a] *Women Writers (1950-1980): A Critical Evaluation* Ed. Mari Evans Gard[en] City, New York: Doubleday, 1984, p.342.

Shlomith Rimmon-Kenan reads Beloved as a double symbol. She is b[oth] personal and psychological and also functions at a collective level. That [is] she is a daughter but also speaks for generations of women lost to slave[ry.] It can be argued her meaning is fragmented just as she fragments [and] explodes at the end of the novel.

Morrison would remind the reader that the opposition of natural a[nd] supernatural is a Western tension. Horvitz (1989) in her response 'Namel[ess] Ghosts: Possession and Dispossession in Beloved' sees Beloved as [a] revenant. She represents not only the dead daughter but also Seth[e's] mother and the women dragged from home onto the slave ships. Ea[ch] mother-daughter has 'loss, perceived abandonment, betrayal and recove[ry'.] This becomes a cycle.

Beloved becomes 'a powerful link in the matrilineal chain that slavery did [its] best to break' (Horvitz, 1989). These memories are ultimately life-giving,[as] they allow Sethe to finally look to the future.

Sethe forgets her mother's language yet these words 'continue to e[xist] inside her as feelings and images that repeatedly emerge as a code that s[he] relies on without realizing it' (Horvitz, 1989). These are animated memori[es] such as the recall of the antelope dance when she feels her baby kick like [an] antelope. These memories do seem tempered by absence – she has ne[ver] seen an antelope and barely remembers her mother but knows it represe[nts] her.

Beloved forces Sethe to interrogate and explore these memories. There i[s a] central irony in that Sethe repeatedly regards her children as her 'best thi[ng'] yet all have been tainted by trauma. Beloved withholds her forgiveness a[nd] in doing so becomes a symbol or embodiment of the past. Repeat[ed] references to chewing, swallowing and laughter suggest a lack of control of the body. It may have been a mechanism to disassociate self from beatings and rapes. There is a deliberate overlap between disremembering and being dismembered.

The end of novel is a contradiction. The author repeats that it is 'not a story to pass on', although the reader cannot ignore the further meaning that we must not pass on or ignore it.

While memory can prevent living in the present, forgetting serves to deny reality. There is both an individual and collective responsibility to remember, a responsibility to honour those who have died and suffered.

TASK: Thematic Concerns

'The conflict between reason and emotion is characteristically Gothic.'

Consider how far you agree with this statement, using support from the text.

Beloved as succubus

Barnett reads Beloved as a succubus combined with a shape-shifting witch from African-American folklore. This figure is a hybrid of cultural traditions.

Succubus

A female demon said to have intercourse with sleeping men, draining their life from them.

Beloved speaks of memories of rape in particular. There are examples of sexual violence emasculating males on the chain gang and commodifying females on the ships and in various forms of entrapment. Sethe's motherhood is desecrated when her milk is taken by adult males. All of these events are traumatic and as Beloved draws them to the surface she becomes an emblem of trauma.

Barnett sees the focus less as gender than race. A number of abuses are listed but there is real terror in Sethe's violence against her own child to prevent her from being 'dirtied' by men in the future. Beloved recalls she is only beloved in the day and named 'bitch in the dark'. Paul D buries his trauma in his rusty tin heart.

Barnett argues that when Beloved has sex with Paul D 'Morrison uses the succubus figure to represent the effects of institutionalized rape under slavery' (Barnett, 1997).

Critical Reading: Barnett, P. 'Figurations of Rape and the Supernatural in Beloved' *PMLA* Vol. 112, No. 3 (Spring 1997): pp.418-427.

This is an unconventional reading which places Beloved as the aggressor. Barnett argues that what takes place in the cold house is rape. Paul D does comment on his powerlessness and it is at this point that his heart opens and he begins to deal with repressed memories such as the chain gang and overhearing his worth.

Beloved drains Sethe's energy as she insists on being fed stories. Barnett (1997) notes: 'Beloved's return to life corresponds to the return of many of Sethe's painful repressed memories of her enslaved past'.

Historically, while commonplace in a system which regarded workers as property, the rape of black women by white plantation owners has been buried in history alongside male rape. Beloved brings memories of assaults to the surface. She is a vampiric figure who sucks life from those she encounters and like these figures there are elements of incestuous, homosexual desire, as in her behaviour in the Clearing.

Beloved is continuously linked with eating and sucking, providing clear echoes of the violations encountered in the institution of slavery by both Sethe and Paul D. Sethe links appetite with annihilation and this is dangerously close to the truth as Beloved starves her towards the end of the narrative. Paul D is shamed by his memories of the chain gang and wearing a bit in his mouth. He feels degraded and emasculated. There is further emasculation when Beloved compels him to have sex seemingly against his will but this does have the result in forcing him to confront his painful memories. Beloved is ultimately cast out by the community working together but there is a threat that she may return 'should the community fail to realize that forgetting, not communal memory, is the condition of traumatic return' (85).

Further Reading: Elizabeth B House 'Toni Morrison's Ghost: The Beloved Who is Not Beloved' in *Studies in American Fiction* (1990)

House reads Beloved as a human figure who can still engender psychic consequences – 'each figure compensates for the loss that the other has sustained' (House, 1990).

If read as human, Sethe's acceptance of Beloved is that of a mother needing love and forgiveness, while Beloved is a vulnerable woman-child needing a family. House looks at Part II to support this reading. In contemplating Beloved's identity, it is suggested that she is a survivor of some form of abuse and entrapment; later in the novel Stamp Paid and Ella link her to rumours of the escape of a young woman held hostage in the house of a white man. House supports this, suggesting that her time spent with education and socialisation would explain her confusion. Her references to water and creeks link to a case of mistaken identity.

The importance of naming

The novel places importance on names and naming. The narrative opens in 1873, almost a decade after the end of the Civil War. Names reflect the varying degrees of independence and the impact of slavery.

Sethe has been named by her mother after her father, a fellow slave. Unlike many of the men at Sweet Home, she has a name provided by family rather than owners. Despite Garner's promotion of a more liberal brand of slave-keeping, this independence is not universal. Paul D has no identity that relates to self, merely the fourth slave named Paul whose name relies on the relationship to a larger group.

Denver's name is also linked to the dominant white population, albeit in a more positive way, as Sethe names her after Amy Denver, the poor runaway who helps her survive and give birth.

Beloved is referenced in a number of ways. Sethe's recollection of her 'crawling already girl' emphasises that although she has not been named there is pride in her achievement and love, despite the drastic action which follows.

Stamp Paid explains why he renounces his birth name of Joshua. His new name is a result of the degradation of slavery. There is grim irony in the name, as he feels the loss of his wife to the sexual whims of his owner means that he has paid his dues in life. The suggestion in the name that he has done enough is not reflected in his actions, as Stamp Paid selflessly continues to help others set up a new life in Ohio. These actions recall his original Biblical namesake Joshua, who was told to lead Israelites to the Promised Land. In his own accounts, ex-slave and abolitionist Frederick Douglass had declared 'there is no modern Joshua' but the novel does have a character who helps others, although later admits to shunning Sethe following her extreme response to the slave catchers.

On a larger scale, re-naming causes a psychological scar. For many, wider family names and tribal links were lost through slavery. This is somewhat illustrated in the figure of Baby Suggs. As Garner drives her to her freedom, he repeatedly calls her Jenny, insisting that he has been told her name is Jenny Whitlow. She reveals that this name has been imposed on her by a previous owner. She explains her preference for Baby Suggs, Suggs after her husband and Baby as this was his term of endearment for her. She has tried to forge a new identity; which Garner dismisses as not appropriate for a mature woman.

While names and heritage had been disrupted, a number of freed ex-slaves saw the opportunity to express themselves and their independence in taking on new names, with many families either changing the spelling of given names or electing the surnames 'Freeman' and 'Freedman'. Baby Suggs is an example of a woman who successfully rejects the names imposed upon her

Ultimately many discover there is a difference between freeing self and claiming self. The sorrow and decline of Baby Suggs is directly linked to the intrusion of the slavecatchers into her yard. Sethe has been allowed to have a name with a family link yet must engage with painful memories to truly reclaim her identity and self.

Post-Structuralism

Studies in post-structuralism concern themselves mainly with language and discourse. Theoretically, whiteness has been 'invisible' in the sense that it is often presented in canonical texts as the normative state of existence.

In *Beloved* white power becomes visible in the physical violence imposed upon enslaved black bodies, particularly Sethe's clump of scars. Post-structuralists would argue that language and discourse serve to create another form of oppression. Some would argue that theories such as post-structuralism can also become a form of oppression, as they reinforce some structures in the process of analysis.

Deconstruction of the text looks at tensions, contradictions and oppositions presented in the text. It relies on a sceptical reading, challenging values and assumptions implicit in a hierarchy of opposites. Cynthia Davis was a key theorist in this area. Her deconstruction looked at mythic structures alongside the gaps and silences which suggests a feminist reading of the struggles experienced by the key characters.

Language gains meaning from the network of associations developed across the text. Fiction can be cyclical and there are repeated themes in a number of Morrison's works. Deconstruction suggests limitless meanings. Morrison writes shunning fixed meaning or resolution. It is difficult to commit to action when meaning is deferred and fragmented. Critics have drawn on anthropological and structural criticism, considering how the symbolism relates to wider society.

Fragmentation in the text

Critical Reading: David Lawrence 'Fleshly Ghosts and Ghostly Flesh: The Word and the Body in Beloved' from *Studies in American Fiction*. 1991

For Lawrence, key themes in the text are the role of memory, the continuity between past and present and the quality of life before and after slavery.

Schoolteacher is representative of the scientific rationality often cited in support of slavery. He categorises the slaves in abstract to make them signify the 'other'. In the text he has so imposed his view on Sethe and Paul D that they only consider self from the perspective of the white gaze. This in turn alienates them, even as free black men and women, from desire and relationships, as there is a distance between body and self.

This fragmentation affects all of the community, resulting in a dissolution of language and body. Throughout there is a rejection of the body. Those who move beyond accepted codes of behaviour are punished, as is seen when the community withhold help, seeing Baby Suggs's party as a display of pride and vanity. Later in the text, women have to begin at the preverbal stage of sound to rebuild the community and banish Beloved.

Language can enslave – both Stamp Paid and Paul D note that black individuals only ever appear in print if an atrocity has been committed – but it can also liberate. Acts of language and storytelling allow Sethe to recover or remember her repressed experiences.

Beloved becomes the embodiment of uninhibited desire. She craves sweets and stories yet she also enables. Paul D's uncontrolled desire taps his repressed memories and unlock his 'rusty tobacco tin' of a heart.

Beloved cannot construct her own self – the 'word-shapes' link to her shifting form. She uses others words as a net or comfort. In sections presented from her point of view the gaps on the page suggest the disintegration of her being. When she demands a merging with Sethe it is a destructive fusion of identity, 'a univocal tyranny'.

The text ends with the conundrum that the heritage of slavery must not 'pass on'. It may need to be forgotten to die away. Enslavement to the past must 'pass on' while at the same time the community must remember and re-articulate in order to re-build.

Beloved as a 'fantastic' text: Todorov and the Fantastic

Tzvetan Todorov (1973) rejects psychoanalytical readings of literature. H
believes that fantasy is based on conflict between the creation of a familia
world and events that cannot be explained by laws governing society o
nature. The reader will finally decide that the event is either an illusion c
the senses or that the event has taken place. This then supports belief in th
marvellous or the uncanny. If marvellous, this acknowledges the element c
supernatural, while uncanny involves the effect of making strange produce
by the distorted or distorting mind of the protagonist.

For Todorov, the fantastic is only part of the work. The ambiguity is resolve
as reader accepts as marvellous or uncanny. One exception is suggested i
The Turn of the Screw by Henry James which sustains ambiguity relating t
the state of mind of the governess at the very end of the narrative. A simila
response is generated when the reader reaches the conclusion of Beloved
Who or what was Beloved? Has she truly left the community?

Further, to be regarded as fantastic the text must comply with at least tw
of the following three conditions:

- The fictional world is one of living people, causing reader to hesitat
  between natural and supernatural explanations.
- Hesitations must be experienced by characters and evident in themes.
- The reader would reject allegorical or poetical interpretations.

Beloved's sudden appearance does find characters such as Paul D assumin
she is a runaway, while Denver has her own beliefs based on the scar tha
she can see on Beloved's neck. There are numerous hesitations and Belove
addresses a number of themes. It could perhaps be argued that the nove
fails to meet the third condition as Beloved can be read as an allegory or a
representing history. However, it can be said that there are certain
fantastic elements throughout the narrative.

The novel does make use of multiple viewpoints, with an emphasis on note
making, and an insistence on comparing points of view to negat
misinterpretation. These aspects undermine the ability to read the text a
an example of Todorov's uncanny, referenced in Part One.

The novel concludes with a potential twist. There is a suggestion that
presence remains, which is then undercut by the insistence that all tha
remains is the weather. The final note throws the acceptance of th
supernatural into uncertainty. This hesitation would suggest a fantastic tex

Beloved as Gothic fiction

Beloved may be considered as supernatural or part of an occult tradition that uses supernatural horror as a reminder of the sacred in the everyday. Here 'sacred' is not necessarily religious but the need to honour and commemorate the many lives lost through the cruelties of the slave trade and the legacy it created.

Beloved shares some features with typical Gothic fiction, in that it exhibits:

> "... *remarkable power to convey a sense of presence; a sense of power, meaning, understanding that explains and naturalised the horror of the past - the terror of temporality - by discovering the sacred within (or at least behind) the fullness of moving time, the Profane.*
>
> **Ronald Schleifer,**
> **discussing the Gothic text *Dracula*. in**
> ***The Trap of the Imagination***

The inhabitants of 124 are defined by closings-in and confinements. They shun the wider community. Beloved is a mysterious figure but there is also the mystery for each character to find what is already there in their memories, what is it that is holding each one back from experiencing life. The past co-exists with the modern world and threatens to engulf it. There is more to know than can ever be known.

The world of the book is presided over by Beloved's presence. The text explicitly draws attention to telling and 'passing on'. As a transcript of memories which will outlast the speakers, the narrative itself may be considered immortal.

The plot of the novel involves the exploration of memories and the use of memory to work through painful experiences. The acceptance of the supernatural alongside the living and the elevated status of reactions are typical Gothic features. The text is marked by a 'stopping short', Sethe's struggle with her memories marked by repetitions and anticipations. The recurrent action of the text is to tell and organise, to make sense of the world. The action is often interrupted as characters attempt to represent experience and record it.

Beloved's presence is amplified through the narration. The search for meaning is constantly constrained by physical reaction to memory, which overwhelms characters and prevents them from moving forward or looking to the future. Despite this, characters understand the need to be resilient and finally, the text and the community assert life against death. Beloved may subvert healthy family relations but the novel does conclude with the community offering support, Denver looking forward to an independent future and Paul D offering to love and support Sethe as she learns to leave the past behind.

The word 'Beloved' is the novel's final text – she is the literal full stop and endnote. It not only reinforces her power and her presence, but also reminds the reader to remember those who have been forgotten and neglected by history.

Throughout the text characters inhabit borders between repression and remembering, moving between sanity and insanity. The characters are seeking meaning from memory and the solution comes through social communication. This search for social and communal origins literally haunts *Beloved* and the Gothic tradition.

The fantastic and the mimetic

Rosemary Jackson (1981) argues that by refusing to acknowledge any form of psychological reading, Todorov is ignoring ideologies present in fantastic literature. She counters that fantasy is deeply concerned with the unconscious and the subconscious. As the world of the unconscious is often resistant to being represented in language this can be located in the gaps, silences, unspoken understanding and difficulty in naming threats.

Jackson (1981) noted that fantasy has been used as a broad term to describe any literature "*which does not give priority to realistic representation... presenting realms 'other' than the human*".

Additionally, fantasy has

"*an obdurate refusal of prevailing definitions of the 'real' or 'possible', a refusal amounting at times to violent opposition*"

(Jackson, 1981)

Beloved begins in the realm of the supernatural. Beloved would seem to have returned from the dead, transgressing the boundaries between life and death, neither fully alive nor decently dead.

If regarded as a fantastic text, Beloved could be grouped with classic Gothic texts such as *Dracula*, *The Strange Case of Dr Jekyll and Mr Hyde*, and *The Picture of Dorian Grey*. These texts share a fear of the monstrous or monstrosity.

Jackson argues that a psychoanalytical reading provides a frame for understanding unconscious thought, Novels can explore the tensions between individual desire and social 'norms' through the 'code' of fantasy. She suggests Todorov's model can be extended if the politics of the form are considered. Rather than focus on structure and formal elements the reader should consider the ideological concerns presented in both form and content.

Jackson also evaluates Todorov's use of the term 'uncanny'. She replaces Todorov's terms of 'marvellous', 'fantastic' and 'uncanny' with the term 'mimetic'. Jackson explains that the marvellous is distanced in to the past while the mimetic claims to imitate external reality. The text should be designed to elicit an emotional response. The mimetic has an authoritative and knowing narrator; *"the fantastic conflates elements of both the marvellous and the mimetic (or realist) ... in the fantastic mode, the narrator shares the reader's uncertainty, constantly questioning and wondering what is 'real' "*.

Fantastic fiction relies on the real to define itself. Denver and Sethe are bewitched from the point where they look beyond plausible explanations for Beloved's appearance. Fantastic fiction highlights the fears of the community relating to the unknown.

TASK: Applying Critical Frameworks: The 'fantastic' and the Gothic

You should consider:

- Evidence of Todorov's 'fantastic' and Jackson's 'mimetic' in the text

- References to uncertainty and doubt when considering Beloved's nature

- How the text creates Gothic borders between past and present, living and dead.

4.3 Psychoanalytical and Gendered Readings

In this section we will;
- *Demonstrate understanding of the significance and influence of the contexts in which literary texts are written and received*
- *Explore connections across literary texts and contexts*
- *To show understanding of how Morrison's choice of form, structure and language shapes meanings.*

Psychoanalytical approaches

In the mid-twentieth century a link was made between fear of vampirism and social taboos regarding sex and death. Building on Freud's earlier discussion of the 'uncanny', the fear of the corruption of the familiar underpins what is uncanny about Beloved.

Jennifer Fitzgerald presents a psychoanalytical criticism of Beloved, while criticising others for isolated readings based on ethnicity and class. There is often a focus on the nuclear family which is not helpful. Fitzgerald looks at the object relations as well as presentations of slavery, the good mother, masculinity and solidarity.

Schapiro does use psychoanalytic theory to look at the breakdown of boundaries. Rage is seen as a 'murderous love'. The excessive dependence of Beloved illustrates the symbiosis of mother and child. Fitzgerald has noted that the mothering is not private. Object relations theory would suggest that social, cultural and political forces are internalised. The text emphasises communal mothering. There is a fissure of the masculine in the uncertainty of Paul D.

For Fitzgerald, Morrison takes us beyond split identity or the splitting of self; 'Beloved dramatises a larger, more powerful sense of a schism in the black community'.

Beloved and Object Relations Theory

Fitzgerald argues Freud's universal but restricted family norm is not a helpful comparison yet there is clearly psychic damage in the text. Fitzgerald outlines 'object relations theory'; 'the psyche is constructed within a wide system of relationships, offering a model of how social, cultural and political forces become internalised' (Fitzgerald, 1993).

Individual Western capitalism privileges individual autonomy in the context of a nuclear family. While damaged by slavery, the women are not only victims but agents within the texts. Paul D is an object and victim as a slave but is subject in discourse on masculinity. Likewise, Sethe is an agent and 'good mother'.

Key discourses in *Beloved* revolve around slavery and meanings of humanity, autonomy and family which are denied through slavery. There is also the concept of the good mother whose sole focus is the well-being of the child. This gives Sethe status and a position of freedom. Paul D wishes to affirm his masculinity. In his wish to share a child with Sethe he has agency.

Object Relations theory is developed from the Kleinian model which examines the infant's conflicting emotions while interacting with the world. Beloved remains a baby, casting her mother as an enemy. Black solidarity is shown through the support network of the Underground railroad and the preaching of Baby Suggs.

Critical Reading:

Fitzgerald, J. 'Selfhood and Community; Psychoanalysis and Discourse in Beloved'. *Modern Fiction Studies* Vol. 39, No. 4(1993).

Beloved has a Pre-Oedipal focus on Sethe which could be linked to Freudian concepts of projection and introjection. Beloved projects her fears and desires on others. Beloved often behaves like a toddler in the developmental stage of attachment. It can be argued that Beloved's seduction of Paul D is a way of keeping Sethe to herself. She can be seen to be caught in an Oedipal crisis. The child normally represses the immediate desire to fit the norms of society and family and will deny certain demands. The child is often taught to consider the needs of others. Beloved does not interact in this way.

Beloved can be read as a real slave or as a ghost, providing evidence of doubling. Beloved feels both love and hate for Sethe, as she is a caregiver but has also abandoned and killed her daughter. Beloved does not realise her separateness in the world, just as a baby thinks it is a unit with its mother. There is a split of the ego – the baby disintegrates into bits.

The novel is pervaded by images of cannibalism, as Sethe is 'eaten by Beloved eyes'. Beloved as infant is angry. She cannot bear her mother's autonomy, just as Beloved the adult does not accept Sethe's reasoning for taking a life.

From the start Sethe insists on her role as a mother. It is an idealised and extreme view of motherhood. Slavery has denied women parental claims. Slavery severed Sethe's bond with her own mother before she carved her own identity, 'her sense of self and of boundaries that self is dangerously weak'.

Beloved does not accept her mother as a separate person. Sethe tries to present the reason why she killed her own baby; 'Not recognising the separateness of her children, Sethe makes life and death decisions for them'. Paul D wants both self-control and free will. He struggles with his masculinity and cannot acknowledge his own vulnerability. He projects this onto Beloved when he finally frees his 'Red Heart'. He projects aspects of self that he does not want to acknowledge onto Sethe, reminding her she isn't an animal. Sixo is more comfortable in his own skin.

Baby Suggs urges the community to forge their own identities after slavery, encouraging a positive engagement with self. Baby Suggs discovers her free self through preaching. Baby Suggs's love extends beyond her family. This inverts the Eurocentric focus on autonomy. She privileges family; *'A man ain't nothing but a man…But a son? Well now, that's somebody'.*

The community should function as an extended mother, offering comfort to those escaping the violence of southern slavery. The community turn away from what they regard as Sethe's arrogance and self-sufficiency. In trying to kill her children she makes a claim for an idealised life. In doing so she resists communal identification and the deprivation of the other ex-slaves. The feast is interpreted as an unfair privilege. They deprive her of the communal 'mothering' when they refuse to sing at Sethe's arrest. They do join together to save Sethe from Beloved. She has had an outrageous claim to the exclusive responsibility to mothering. Now they offer 'extended social network of care and support'.

'Beloved's exposition of communal mother offers an alternative to the individualism and autonomy privileged by classical psychoanalysis'. For nineteen years, communal solidarity is withheld from Sethe. The community mothering takes place in the social sphere of everyday life. Slavery had caused one group of people to be defined as the property of another Humanity was not recognised. White becomes a metaphor for merging Baby Suggs craves colour in her final years.

The community can offer solidarity and support. It is based on helping and sharing. Social relations nurture the individual's sense of self. Denver, Sethe and Paul D move from repressive isolation to a more developed sense of self Self-healing is provided by a community of survivors.

Further Reading: Kristin Boudreau (1995) 'Pain and the Un-making of Self in Toni Morrison's *Beloved*' from *Contemporary Literature*.

Boudreau suggests that the novel sets out to challenge traditional models of suffering, whether they be Keat's Romanticism and 'negative capability' or the pain expressed in the Blues. Throughout the novel language and narrative structure are dismantled and undermined by the torture of slavery.

The influence of these traditions is seen, as when Sethe presents her romantic vision of Sweet Home. She sees the beauty of the trees before briefly recalling that young men's corpses hang from them. Sethe fails to articulate all that she has seen.

Throughout the novel, Beloved becomes a model of the self. This is also flawed as she is unstable, both in body and language. Morrison argues that to be human is 'to occupy an ever-shifting identity'.

TASK: Evaluating Critical Interpretations

Take one of the psychoanalytical and gendered readings in this section and attempt to argue against this.

You should consider:
• Alternative interpretations of textual examples provided in the reading
• Alternative explanations for characterisation or Morrison's use of language.

4.4 Postmodern and Post-colonial Readings

In this section we will;
- *Demonstrate understanding of the significance and influence of the contexts in whi* *literary texts are written and received*
- *Explore connections across literary texts and contexts*
- *To show understanding of how Morrison's choice of form, structure and langua* *shapes meanings.*

Postmodern Approaches

Rafael Perez-Torres sees the text as post-modern. He challenges the idea the objectivity of history. The subject is fluid and fragmented. The subjectivities blur culture and society, male and female, and history a fiction.

Absences in the text are considered. The exploitation and denial of bla cultural identity makes itself a powerful presence in the gaps and absenc in the text. He feels Morrison's text does share some characteristics wi European postmodernism, such as the crossing of styles, mix of genres a multiple perspectives. The novel creates 'an aesthetic identity out absence' (Torres, 1993).

Beloved as a postmodern novel

Critical Reading:

Pérez-Torres, R. 'Knitting and Knotting the Narrative Thread – Beloved as Postmodern Novel'. *Modern Fiction Studies* Vol.39, No. 4 (1993).

Perez-Torres argues that the novel transforms an 'essential absence into powerful presence'. Voice and identity are created from 'experiences exploitation, marginalisation and denial'.

Postmodern characteristics include oral and written discourses, movemer from third person to omniscient to interior monologue, and the iteration a re-iteration of words and phrases. The novel is concerned with th production and meaning of language. The text also provides mythic a folkloric elements.

Critic Henry Louis Gates had argued that if a black writer has to use language where blackness signifies absence, the construction of an identi is constrained. Morrison addresses this by using elements of Western a non-Western literary production.

The novel opens detailing death, absences and long-gone sons. Sethe suspended between a traumatic past and an uncertain future. The ghosts the past are trying to assert themselves in the fictional present. Morris warns readers this is 'not a story to pass on'. It cannot be repeated yet also should not be forgotten.

Throughout the novel we can trace the interplay of presence and absence, acceptance and rejection, appearance and disappearance as the boundaries of life and death are blurred. Baby Suggs is dead but her presence is ley in the narrative and prompts Denver to take the final saving action of involving the community.

Slavery is the absence of power and self-determination. Slaves lack a language and a homeland. Slavery relies on commodity and exchange. This is not only on the part of the owners, but on the part of the abolitionists who wish to promote a cause. The women have channels of exchange which are social and personal; these seek to replace the market exchange.

For Baby Suggs, colour is a richness that she craves in later life. There are layers of discourse as the text has serious political, social and cultural implications. Play would be rebellion. While the characters rarely play, the novel plays with words and their wider political and cultural meanings. Elsewhere in the guide, the competing signs of the 'At Yo' Service' figurine in place in the home of the abolitionist Bodwins provided 'a comprehensive critique of the commercial, racist and potentially violent nature of the dominant social order'.

The cup of loose change becomes equated with the service of the black population and the kneeling figure recalls servitude, while the boy's contorted neck recalls a lynching. This is troubling sign as Denver makes arrangements to join the household as a servant. This is one example of Morrison foregrounding relationships of language and power.

The opening lines note gap between the narrative present and the fictional past. Sethe cannot find a language. She has become an agent 'subject to the tyranny of history'. Paul D wants to write a legacy with her by having a child. Paul tells her they need a tomorrow. Beloved's story needs to be concluded to enable new stories to begin. The final word is an inscription.

The text can be seen as a pastiche, 'a liberating technique which frees the signifier from a fixed frame of reference'. The narrative moves through a range of styles – oral, preliterate, journalistic, modern prose – so it 'becomes a metanarrative at play in the field of the novel'.

The novel deals with those who have been historically decentred, creating a communal voice alongside modernism. It is driven by a 'decentring impulse'. Throughout the novel the power of naming and re-naming is highlighted.

Absences in *Beloved*

Critical Reading:

Pérez-Torres, R.
'Between
Presence and
Absence:
Beloved,
Postmodernism,
and Blackness' in
*A Casebook on
Beloved*. Ed.
William Andrews
and Nellie Y.
McKay (Oxford
University Press,
1999).

In a further essay, Torres provided an examination of the novel through a postmodern frame. The characters and communities 'transform absences into a powerful presence'.

The novel opens with facts followed by a series of losses. There is evidence of missing ancestors and descendants. The text ends with a request not to 'pass on'. Rejection and acceptance co-exist as this is a story that should 'neither be forgotten or remembered'. Demarcation between life and death is blurred throughout the narrative.

Action is driven by absences. The absence of Garner prompts the escape, the absence of her other children drives pregnant Sethe on and the absence of Halle leads her to stay at 124.

It is a society of commodity and exchange. Sethe eventually tells her story in social and personal exchanges. The text moves between modern and postmodern. Throughout there is a pun on colour. Baby Suggs desperately seeks colour in the later stages of her life yet all have suffered due to a society which classifies according to skin colour.

Gates introduces the term signifiyin(g). This refers to the process of playing with codes which have serious implications. Torres uses this to argue that the text has a more serious meaning than other postmodern texts. An example can be Denver's moment of pause looking at the '*At Yo' Service*' figurine. This is unstable – she is the home of abolitionists looking for work. On one hand they support the black community; on the other they have a figure of a young black boy with his head thrown back in a hideous and painful way being used to keep the small change required for odd jobs.

In a more damaging way, schoolteacher uses language to violate. Bodies are written on through hangings, burning and mutilations. His final violation to use words to debase others and compare them to animals. He shows that power belongs to those who define. The absence of power leads to renegotiating and re-signifying signs. An example is Sethe's chokecherry tree.

The text presents a tension between two cultures. For some Americans there is the elegiac invocation of a lost culture. From an African perspective loss in brought into existence through words. Sethe's body is a constant marker and text. She has served as property while a slave – she is still property to a degree when Paul D wants a baby and a legacy through her.

The various forms within the narrative can be read as a postmodern pastiche. The novel seeks to create uncertainty to open up reading. Pastiche does serve to challenge history as a master narrative. Storytelling forms part of the story, as with the various versions of Denver's birth. This is told 3 times. *Beloved* makes overt connections between language and power.

Barbara Christian notes that Morrison read myths from a variety of cultures in preparation for writing the novel. Her focus was on revenants or the returning dead. She is disappointed to note that many critics limit themselves to psychoanalytical readings, with limited awareness of traditional, African and folkloric influences. She concludes both African and American influences are present, given the multi-layered nature of Morrison's work. It could be seen as the myth of eternal return, based on the longing of a people.

The Middle Passage brought nationalities together through suffering. The novel demonstrates the importance of the community of memory. It can be healing, as when Paul D informs Sethe that Halle did not abandon her but was driven mad.

Re-memory can be regarded as every consideration of an event. This is achieved through re-creating and re-membering what has happened. Memory is creative. It is not necessarily consistent.

What does remain is that infanticide is viewed as taboo. Sethe's actions are not sentimentalized. Denver is the only child who knows her mother. All of the community have been separated from the motherland. The mother who loves is also the mother who destroys.

The text also presents images of currency, from Denver's 'nickel life' to Paul D's 'worth'. The question which remains is the point at which love becomes obsession. Slavery made slaves aware of their worth, which in turn had implications for how freed slaves treated each other. Sethe sees herself as embodied in the milk that was stolen from her. The text is not sentimental. The community attacks Baby Suggs due to guilt over their own gluttony. Morrison invites the African-American communities to judge the more negative elements of early freed society too.

Post-colonial Approaches

Critical Reading:

Keenan, S. (1993)

'Four Hundred Years of Silence': Myth, History and Motherhood in Toni Morrison's Beloved'.

Keenan clearly locates the novel in a post-colonial context. While a p[...] colonial nation itself, America is also implicated in colonial oppression, b[...] with genocide of indigenous populations and enslavement.

Keenan suggests the relationship between Sethe and Beloved provides[...] analogy to the links between African-Americans and history. This can[...] appreciated alongside the metonymic relationship of mother and daugh[...] which slavery tried to destroy.

Beloved can be seen as an exemplary revision of past history. Morri[...] shows motherhood and female resistance as central, 'the heart of[...] exploration if the processes of memory, recovery and representation[...] African American history'. The novel articulates the struggle to fin[...] language which can speak about the past. It seeks to extend the limit[...] traditional slave narratives.

For Keenan (1993), *Beloved* is 'a complex metaphor for black Ameri[...] relationship with its enslaved past'. The text provides a site for[...] contestation of the ways that the past has been erased by or subsum[...] within the historical discourse of the hegemonic culture'.

The text is both metaphoric and metonymic. Homi Bhabha argues t[...] metonymy is a preferable trope for the study of post-colonial literature;[...]

'Metonymy can be employed to symptomatize the social, cultural [...] political forces that traverse those texts'. The focus on the maternal can [...] provide a metaphor for the population's relation to slavery. Throughout[...] text there is an analogy between feeding and storytelling. In places [...] pushes empirical history, as in Sethe's miraculous escape from slavery w[...] heavily pregnant. Sadly, this was not in evidence in history.

New Historicists

Ashraf Rushdy as a New Historicist feels Morrison's concern is with the 'history of history'. The history of slavery is reclaimed from the point of view of the black female slave. Her wider discussion centres on the story of Margaret Garner, Morrison's use of Camille Bishop's text *'The Harlem Book of the Dead' and* the use of James Van Der Zee's pictures as inspiration.

Signifyin(g) in *Beloved*

Critical Reading:

Rushdy, A. 'Daughters Signifyin(g) History: The Example of Toni Morrison's Beloved'. *American Literature* Vol.64, No. 3 (1992).

African-American texts insist on interdependence of past and present. It is a political act, 'a revisioning of the past as it is filtered through the present' (Rushdy, 1992). Garner's story was detailed in *The Liberator*, 1856 and The *Annual Report* of the American Anti-Slavery Society 1856.

In January 1856, Margaret Garner escaped her owner Archibald Gaines. She travelled from Kentucky, crossed the Ohio river and reached Cincinnati. Margaret cut her beloved daughter's throat and tried to kill the other children and herself. She found this action preferable to the dehumanisation of slavery. Morrison found something selfless in this. It was a famous story which circulated even as late as 1892 to criticise and warn about slavery.

Morrison presents 'reconstructive memory'. There are concerns with transmission. Beloved has some hopefulness. It does not have the orthodoxy of victimhood. Morrison fears that slavery could be part of 'collective amnesia' as nations want to forget. This is not a novel about slavery although it is about an ex-slave.

The novel remains ambivalent. All want to forget yet they need to remember at the same time. *Beloved* as a novel is 'a requiem that is a resurrection' (Rushdy,1992).

Beloved has an unforgiving view of the past, while Denver embraces the past. Beloved is an embodiment of the past – she highlights that others must remember to forget. Originally Morrison was going to focus on Denver's story. Denver 'is the site of hope'.

Morrison writes 'from a double perspective of accusation and hope'. There are two sides to the debate. Slavery had led to the 'infantilisation' of adult slaves; internal communities, family structures and protectors allowed for rich, coherent lives beyond slavery.

The representation of Beloved has been contested. She may be one of history's anonymous victims. Beloved remembers victimization while establishing healing powers of community. The novel enacts repossession and historical recovery. The signifyin(g) or reinterpretation of the murder takes place when Sethe realises the responsibilities lie with the institution of slavery and the slave owners.

Collective Selves

> **Further Reading: April Lidinsky 'Prophesising Bodies: Calling for a Politics of Collectivity in Toni Morrison's 'Beloved'** from Plasa, C. and Ring, B.J. *The Discourse of Slavery: Aphra Behn to Toni Morrison* (1994)
>
> In this essay, Lidinsky looks particularly at the characters of Baby Suggs and Paul D. She looks at how collectively communities can work to reclaim identity.

Baby Suggs can be seen as a political centre in the novel. Having been a station master at 124, she then develops her own belief system and makes a call to the community to reimagine the self. Her self-appointment as a preacher and the gatherings in the Clearing present the possibility of collective political action. Baby Suggs draws on the established churches but also presents ideas of subjectivity and reconstruction.

Lidinsky notes the foregrounding of matrilineal aspects and slavery in the novel but turns her attention in the critical essay to the black male subject. She examines the role of communication in Paul D's escape from the chain gang. Talk could have betrayed the men yet the use of song and communicating through the chain transforms 'the very device that keeps them partitioned into a mechanism for collective agency'.

The chain emphasises the bodily effects of enslavement. There are links to treatment as animals and also the iron will that it took to endure the experience. History inhabits their bodies yet it also galvanizes them to move.

Lidinsky would agree with Morrison's own critical approach, that while postmodern criticism arrived just at a time when subjugated people are finding their voice, it can still provide some support in texts looking at outmoded notions of identity. Sethe fails to recognise self as a slave and mistakenly believes she is defined as a mother, with her children her 'best thing'. As the novel closes, Paul D encourages Sethe to be her 'own best thing'.

Appendices

Sample Assessment Tasks

Below are the types of questions you may be asked to answer as part of the Edexcel examination. For the Prose assessment you will be comparing Beloved with another text in the Supernatural option. The paired text is one chosen from *Dracula* by Bram Stoker, *The Picture of Dorian Gray* by Oscar Wilde and *The Little Stranger* by Sarah Waters.

EDEXCEL A LEVEL 9ET02 PROSE

In your answer you must consider the following:

- the writers' methods
- links between the texts
- the relevance of contextual factors.

a) Compare the ways in which the writers of your two chosen texts create **a sense of fear** in their works. You must relate your discussion to relevant contextual factors.

b) Compare the ways in which **settings are created and used** by the writers of your two chosen texts. You must relate your discussion to relevant contextual factors.

c) Compare the ways in which the writers of your two chosen texts convey **the threat or presence of death.**

d) Compare the ways in which the writers of your two chosen texts **make use of significant locations** in their texts.

e) Compare the ways in which the writers of your two chosen texts present **characters who experience anxiety**.

f) Compare the ways in which the writers of your two chosen texts **examine violence**. You must relate your discussion to relevant contextual factors.

EDEXCEL AS LEVEL 8ET02 PROSE

a) Compare the ways in which the writers of your two chosen texts present **cruelty.**

b) Compare the ways in which the writers of your two chosen texts present **masculinity**.

urther Reading

keland, L.   'Remodelling the Model Home in Uncle Tom's Cabin and Beloved' *American Literature* Vol. 64, No. 4 (Winter 1992). Duke University Press.

rnett, P.   'Figurations of Rape and the Supernatural in Beloved' *PMLA* Vol. 112, No. 3 (Spring 1997): pp.418-427.

udreau, K.   'Pain and the Unmaking of Self in Toni Morrison's 'Beloved'. *Contemporary Literature.* Vol.36, No. 3 (Autumn, 1995): pp.447-465. University of Wisconsin Press.

endese, P.   'Making Silence Speak: Toni Morrison and the Beloved Community' in *The Power of Memory in Democratic Politics.* Boydell and Brewer, 2014. pp.83-103

endese, P.   *The Power of Memory in Democratic Politics.* Boydell and Brewer. Woodridge, United Kingdom.

vis, C.   'Self, Society and Myth in Toni Morrison's Fiction'. *Contemporary Literature* Vol. 23, No. 3 (1982): pp. 323-342. University of Wisconsin Press.

urkin, A.   'Object Written, Written Object: Slavery, Scarring, and Complications of Authorship in Beloved'. *African American Review.* Vol. 41, No. 3 (2006): pp.541-556. Indiana State University.

tzgerald, J.   'Selfhood and Community; Psychoanalysis and Discourse in Beloved'. *Modern Fiction Studies* Vol. 39, No. 4(1993): pp.669-687. John Hopkins University Press.

ouse, E.   'Toni Morrison's Ghost: The Beloved is Not Beloved'. *Studies in American Fiction.* Vol. 18, No. 1 (Spring, 1990): pp. 17-26.

orvitz, Deborah   "Nameless Ghosts: Possession and Dispossession in 'Beloved' ". *Studies in American Fiction*, Vol. 17, no. 2 (Autumn, 1989) p.157-168

eenan, S.   'Four Hundred Years of Silence': Myth, History and Motherhood in Toni Morrison's Beloved'. *Recasting the World: Writing After Colonialism* Ed. Jonathan White (1993). Baltimore: John Hopkins University Press.

umholz, L.   'The Ghosts of Slavery: Historical Recovery in Toni Morrison's Beloved'. *African American Review* Vol. 26, No. 3 (Autumn, 1992): pp.395-408. Indiana State University.

wrence, D.   'Fleshly Ghost and Ghostly Flesh: The Word and Body in Beloved'. *Studies in American Fiction.* Vol.19, No. 2 (Autumn 1991): pp.189-201. John Hopkins University Press.

Lidinsky, A.   'Prophesying bodies: calling for a politics of collectivity in Toni Morrison 'Beloved' in The Discourse of Slavery (1994): pp.191-216. London.

Pérez-Torres, R.   'Knitting and Knotting the Narrative Thread – Beloved as Postmodern Nove *Modern Fiction Studies* Vol.39, No. 4 (1993): pp.689-707

Pérez-Torres, R.   'Between Presence and Absence: Beloved, Postmodernism, and Blackness' *A Casebook on Beloved*. Ed. William Andrews and Nellie Y. McKay (Oxfor University Press, 1999).

Peterson, C.   'Beloved's Claim'. *MFS Modern Fiction Studies* Vol. 52, No. 3 (Autumn 2006 pp.548-569. John Hopkins University Press.

Rimmon-Kenan, S.   'Narration, Doubt, Retrieval: Toni Morrison's Beloved'. *Narrative* Vol.4, No (May, 1996): pp.109-123. Ohio State University Press.

Rushdy, A.   'Daughters Signifyin(g) History: The Example of Toni Morrison's Beloved *American Literature* Vol.64, No. 3 (1992): pp.567-597. Duke University Pres

CPSIA information can be obtained
at www.ICGtesting.com
Printed in the USA
BVHW032152121022
649354BV00009B/66